Art, Craft, Design

CLODAGH HOLAHAN
MAUREEN ROCHE

GILL & MACMILLAN

Published in Ireland by
Gill & Macmillan Ltd
Goldenbridge
Dublin 8
with associated companies throughout the world
www.gillmacmillan.ie
© Clodagh Holahan and Maureen Roche 1993
© Artwork, Gill & Macmillan 1993
0 7171 2031 7

Editorial Consultant: Roberta Reeners
Design: Fergus O'Keeffe
Artwork: Alanna Corballis/Niche Design
Photography: Rod Tuach and Denis Baker
Picture Research: Anne-Marie Ehrlich
Cover Design: Graham Thew
Index compiled by Helen Litton
Print origination in Ireland by
Seton Music Graphics Ltd, Bantry, Co. Cork
Printed in the E.C.

A catalogue record is available for this book from the British Library.

Cover painting: *Pottery,* Patrick Caulfield, The Tate Gallery, London

Photocopying
prohibited
by law

For our children
Jessica
and
Etaoin, Róisín, Aoife and Senan

To our husbands, Billy Gardiner and Luke Cody, our thanks for their support and patience.
To our friends, relatives and school colleagues for their co-operation, with thanks to our 'special' artists, models and helpers: Etaoin, Róisín and Aoife Holahan, Senan Gardiner, Anne Marie McEvoy, Marie Marthe Viet, Joan Tobin, Katie Dunne, Catherine Brennan, Mary Brennan-Holahan.
Special thanks to Kilkenny VEC Ballyhale Vocational School, Co. Kilkenny and St Brigid's College, Callan, Co. Kilkenny for accommodating us and allowing us to use our students' work.
Many thanks to all the teachers who offered comments and suggestions.
Thanks are due to our editor, Roberta Reeners, who accepted a marathon task in dealing with us, as well as our manuscript.
Thanks to our designer, Fergus O'Keeffe, and to the staff at Gill & Macmillan, particularly Hubert Mahony and Mairead Peters.
Thanks are also due to Kinealys Art and Office Supplies, Patrick Street, Kilkenny.

Acknowledgments

The publishers express their thanks to the following artists, crafts people, organisations and individuals for their assistance: Nicholas Mosse Pottery, Paula Hicks/National Gallery of Ireland, Des Dillon, Jackie McKenna, Sculpture Society of Ireland, Irish Wildbird Conservancy, Guinness Ireland Ltd, An Óige, Bord Iascaigh Mhara, Virgin Megastore Dublin, Martin Gale, Pauline Bewick, Bernadette Madden, Stoneware Jackson Pottery, Sligo Pottery, Brian Keogh Pottery, Gorta, Credit Union of Ireland, Kilkenny Shops, Robert Ballagh, Brian Bourke, Louis le Brocquy, John Behan, Michael Fairclough, Bryan Organ, Edward Bawden, Real Ireland Ltd, Aer Lingus, Coca-Cola Ireland, Levis Ireland, U2/Principle Management, The Philatelic Bureau, Erin Soups, Wilson Hartnell, Mars Ireland, Dublin Wax Museum, F. E. McWilliam, Patricia McKenna, Bill Woodrow, Bridget Riley, Mary Lee Murphy, Patricia Walsh-Smith, Charles Smith, John Nuttgens, Kenealys Art and Office Supplies/Kilkenny, Alice Power, Ignatius O'Neill, Taylor Galleries.

For permission to reproduce photographs and colour transparencies, acknowledgment is made to the following: Robert Harding Picture Library, et archive, Rod Tuach, Luke Cody, Clodagh Holahan, Maureen Roche, J. Allan Cash, Don Sutton International Photo Library, Slide File, The Kobal Collection, The Bridgeman Art Library, Ancient Art and Architecture, National Gallery of Ireland, National Gallery/London, The Tate Gallery, Rijksmuseum/Amsterdam, The Royal Collection/St James' Palace, Archive Karg/Baumeister Switzerland, Zefa Picture Library, Rex Features, Panache Studios Ltd, SONY, Eaglemoss Publications, National Gallery of Scotland, Butler Gallery/Kilkenny, Michael Holford, Robert Estall Photographs © Angela Fisher and Carol Beckwith, Werner Forman Archive, A. Sanderson & Sons, Heather Angel, Angelo Hornak Library, British Museum, Victoria and Albert Museum, CCL Galleries, 8 Dover Street, London W1X 3PJ, ARCAID, Haags Gementemuseum/Holland, Albertina Graphic Collection/Vienna, Giraudon, Louvre/Paris, Henry Moore Foundation, Scala, Courtauld Institute Galleries/London, The Mansell Collection, M. C. Escher Foundation/Baarn Holland, Penrose Collection/Lee Miller, Glasgow Museums: Art Gallery and Museum/Kelvingrove, Museum of Modern Art, New York/© Mrs Simon Guggenheim Fund, Musées Nationaux/France, Fine Art Society/London, Redfern Gallery/London, Bruno Munari, Angela Murphy, Kodak Museum at The National Museum of Photography, Film and TV/Bradford, BPCC/Aldus Archive, Gernsheim Collection, University of Austin, Texas, Library of Congress, EV Research, Office of Public Works, Shambles Art Gallery/Belfast, Lissan Gallery, Barry Friedman Gallery Ltd.

Contents

Preparatory Work

Preparatory Work refers to the sketches, investigations, experiments, attempts and plans that precede the student's finished work.

Support Studies

Support Studies may be either written or visual. They should both relate to and reinforce each area of a project or theme.

Support Studies may be derived from both the history and appreciation of Art, Craft, Design. Students may include descriptions of visits to galleries, museums, craft shops and workshops (e.g. potteries, foundries, stone cutters' yards, weavers' sheds). Such experiences may be illustrated with your own photographs or sketches, along with brief captions. Brochures and other back-up material are also valid.

Support Studies sources

postcards; packaging (sweet papers to cardboard boxes); calendars; wrapping paper (general/birthdays /Christmas); magazines/comics; carrier bags; newspapers; book jackets/book promotions; brochures; video covers/film advertisements; catalogues; record albums/CDs/cassettes; leaflets; reference books/books in general; handouts; Art, Craft, Design books; posters; photocopies of any of the above (subject to any photocopying regulations)

Valid material includes any visual or written work which relates to the project and the required area of study, through the chosen theme, from an historic and/or working point of view.

Introduction

One of the most exciting subjects you can study is **Art, Craft, Design.** You will see examples of it everywhere you look. It is part of what we are, the way we live and the things we do.

It is found in the **places** in which we live.

It is in the **clothes** we wear.

You will see elements of design in the **cars** we drive.

It is in the **food** we eat.

It can be seen in the **packaging** and **labelling** of these foods and in most of the other products we buy. Art, Craft, Design is also a big part of sales and marketing, since it is used in the design and visual presentation of a product.

Observe and Discuss

Choose a common object — anything from a car to a chocolate bar. Look at the design of the packaging and discuss the ways in which this tries to attract the consumer.

The covers of **records, tapes** and **CDs** use art and design.

It is part of the **film and TV industries** and can be seen in **special effects,** costumes, sets, make-up, composition and lighting. The list is almost endless!

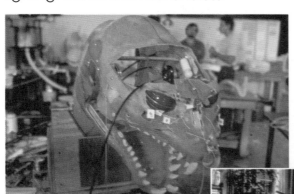

These special effects were designed for the films *Ghostbusters* (left and centre) and *Mutronics* (right).

We can see design in **nature** — in the great outdoors.

Pottery designed in Kilkenny by Nicholas Mosse.

And what could be more natural than reflecting the patterns and designs of nature in the things we use?

Pottery bowl and tall jug designed by the Welsh potter, John Nuttgens.

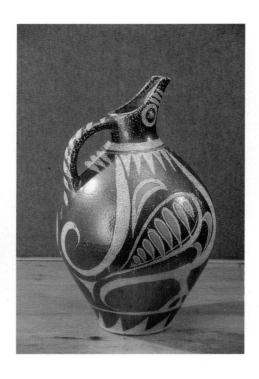

We are completely surrounded by art, craft and design as we go about our daily lives.

Many kinds of art

What about the 'art' we see in museums and galleries? This is often called **fine art** — paintings, drawings, sculptures.

Of course, art existed long before there were museums and art galleries. **Cave paintings** are a good example of this. They were done by early humans to capture the spirit of the world around them, especially the animals they hunted. **Tomb paintings** often showed the land and property of the dead person. By showing scenes from the life of the deceased, it was thought such things would be useful in the next life.

This painting of a bison on the wall of a cave at Altamira in Spain was made about 15,000 years ago.

An Egyptian nobleman and noblewoman hunt birds along the River Nile in this tomb painting from 1425 BC.

Virgin and the Saints by Andrea Mantegna (c.1431–1506) is known as a triptych (three wooden panels). It is in the Basilica di San Veno, Verona, Italy.

Some of the earliest fine art pictures were **religious paintings**. They were often commissioned by religious leaders who displayed them in churches to teach people about their religion. Some of these paintings were almost like comic strips, as most people could neither read nor write.

One of the greatest religious paintings is *The Last Judgment*. This huge **fresco** was painted between 1536 and 1541 by the Italian artist, Michelangelo (1475 – 1564), during the **Renaissance**. This was a time of a great revival of the arts and learning in Europe between 1400 – 1600. *The Last Judgment* (below) can still be seen on the altar wall of the Sistine Chapel in Rome. A fresco (from the Italian word for 'fresh') had to be painted onto freshly-prepared wet plaster which soaked up the paint as it dried.

The image at the right, often called *The Creation,* is on the ceiling of the Sistine Chapel.

Mythological scenes were also very popular during the Renaissance. These were paintings based on the lives of ancient Greek and Roman gods and goddesses.

Primavera, Sandro Botticelli (c.1445–1510). Panel. Uffizi Gallery, Florence.

The Merchant George Gisze, Hans Holbein the Younger (c.1497–1542). State Museum, Berlin.

Wealthy people often commissioned paintings of themselves and the members of their families. They used these **portraits** to decorate the walls of their fine mansions.

Charles V on Horseback, Titian (c.1485–1576). Oil on canvas. Prado, Madrid.

The great Renaissance painter, Leonardo da Vinci (1452–1519), used drawings as a way of investigating scientific subjects. He also made many drawings in preparation for his paintings.

Drawings by Leonardo showing his design ideas for war machines.

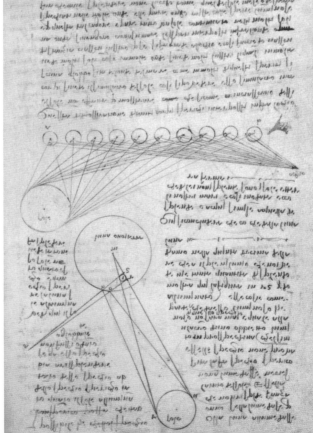

A page from Leonardo's notebooks with his thoughts about the sun and moon.

Leonardo did many studies of natural history, like this cluster of oak leaves and acorns.

Great battles were recorded in paintings.

The Battle of San Romano, Paolo Uccello (c.1397–1475). A painted panel, probably from the Medici Palace in Venice. National Gallery, London.

So were weddings.

The Jewish Bride, Rembrandt Van Rijn (1606–1669). Oil on canvas. Rijksmuseum, Amsterdam.

The Dutch liked to show the interiors of their homes.

The Music Lesson, Jan Vermeer (1632–1675).
The Royal Collection, St James' Palace, London.

Genre was an art form which showed scenes from everyday life. It was particulary popular in Holland in the 17th century and made famous by Vermeer.

Interior of a Dutch House, Pieter de Hoogh (1629–1684). National Gallery, London.

At one time, landscape scenes were simply used as backgrounds for subjects such as portraits, battles and mythological scenes. Early in the nineteenth century, many artists began to paint outdoor scenes. **Landscape paintings** then became very popular in their own right.

The Haywain, John Constable (1776–1837). Oil on canvas. National Gallery, London. Constable was one of the first artists to paint out-of-doors, using the landscape as his subject matter.

One famous group of painters who did most of their work outdoors was called the **Impressionists**. They worked towards the end of the nineteenth century. They were famous for their experiments with colour and natural light, as can be seen in this painting by the Irish Impressionist, William Leech.

The Goose Girl (A View of Quimperle), William Leech (1881–1968). National Gallery of Ireland.

Shape, colour and pattern fascinated the Swiss painter, Paul Klee (1879-1940), and the Irish artist, Mainie Jellett (1897-1944).

Midtropical Landscape, Paul Klee (1879 - 1940). Private Collection.

Cubist Decoration, Mainie Jellett (1897–1944). Oil on canvas. National Gallery of Ireland.

Some paintings are purely decorative. Others make a strong comment on the society of the time. *Autumn Cannibalism* is by the Surrealist painter Salvador Dali. In it he tells of the horrors of the Spanish Civil War which engulfed his country from 1936 to 1939.

Signpost

See *Guernica,* pages 150-151.

Autumn Cannibalism, Salvador Dali (1904–1989). Tate Gallery, London.

Sculpture was used mainly for memorials.

The O'Connell Monument, John Henry Foley (1818–1874). Bronze. Dublin.

A bronze statue of the writer Balzac by the French sculptor Auguste Rodin (1840–1917). Paris.

Famine Statue, Edward Delaney. St Stephen's Green, Dublin.

The Iwo Jima Statue, Felix de Weldon. This statue depicts one of the most famous moments in World War II when American Marines took control of the Pacific island of Iwo Jima. It stands in Washington DC. The Capitol and the Washington Monument are in the background.

Photography

Photography is probably the most recent of all art forms. It quickly became a popular way of showing people, scenes and objects. Photography caused great worry for many artists in the late nineteenth and early twentieth centuries. Portrait painters were particularly concerned. But some people learned to exploit photography and created an art form through their use of the camera.

A formal photographic portrait of the Hiller family around 1885. Victoria and Albert Museum, London.

Fashion photography came into its own in the 1960s.

Advances in technology have made space photography possible.

The Basic Elements of Art, Craft, Design

From what you have seen so far, you should realise that there is more to Art, Craft, Design than meets the eye. It is about so many things — investigating, exploring, analysing, recording, expressing and communicating. It involves an ability to appreciate, evaluate and criticise.

To help you cover a vast range of topics, we will start with the basic elements of Art, Craft, Design.

These are:

- **Colour**
- **Pattern and Shape**
- **Line**
- **Texture**
- **Form and Space**

A knowledge of these elements will give you the freedom to tackle any project.

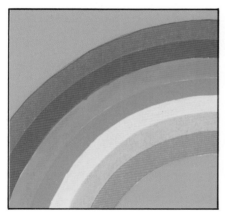

Colour

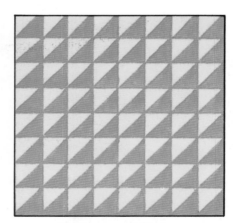

Pattern and Shape

Texture

Form and Space

Line

Colour

Support Studies

Our bodies react to colour every day, even though we are not aware of it. Some colours say: 'Relax. Take it easy'. Others say: 'Wake up! Get going!' We are usually unaware of these messages, but we obey them subconsciously.

Red has a stimulating effect on us. Blue and green have relaxing effects, making us feel calmer and more rested.

A good example of colour used in marketing and advertising can be seen in fast-food stores. Very often, they use combinations of red and yellow to keep us on the move. On the other hand, aeroplane manufacturers want their customers to feel safe and relaxed. That is why they use blue, green and cream in aeroplane interiors.

International surveys have shown that most people react in the same way to different colours. Their nationality, language or level of intelligence seems to make no difference to their reactions. This research can tell us a number of important things about ourselves. It can tell whether we are calm or aggressive, whether we are confident or timid, whether we are conservative or rebellious, contented or ambitious. Colour reactions can even tell whether we run the risk of a heart attack! They cannot, however, indicate one's level of intelligence.

A fast-food restaurant.

An aeroplane interior.

A market in Malaysia.

Skeins of dyed Indian silk.

How do you react to the colours in these photographs? What do the colours say?

Support Studies

What is colour?

Colour is the result of the breakdown of white light into its single colour elements by using a glass prism. These colour elements are red, orange, yellow, green, blue, indigo and violet. They are the colours of the rainbow.

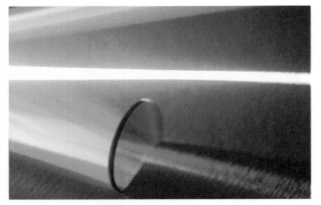

Breaking white light into single colours using a prism.

It was the British physicist, Sir Isaac Newton (1647–1727), who first showed that natural white light is a combination of all the colours of the visible light spectrum.

Raindrops can also act as prisms and thus can create rainbows.

To have colour, three factors must be satisfied.

1. **Light** — You must have light, either natural daylight or artificial light.
2. **Surface** — Without a surface, there can be no colour.
3. **Eye** — It is the eye which translates pure light waves into colour.

Suggested Assignments

1. Collect examples of pictures, advertisements, cards etc. which are full of colour. The pictures have to shout 'Colour!', as in the examples on the following pages.
2. Collect examples of pictures of interiors which have either a stimulating or calming effect on us. Think about schools, hospitals, department stores, living rooms, kitchens etc.
3. Find other examples of interiors — train, plane and bus stations, restaurants, hotels etc.

Observe and Discuss

Look at the work of these artists. Note their use of colour. Look at other paintings in this book and comment on the artists' use of colour.

Landscape at Murnau 1909, Wassily Kandinsky (1866–1944). Oil on paper. Kunstmuseum, Dusseldorf.

Circular Forms, Robert Delaunay (1885–1941). Oil on canvas. ©Solomon R. Guggenheim Foundation, New York.

The Vision after the Sermon, Paul Gauguin (1848-1903). Oil on canvas. National Gallery of Scotland, Edinburgh.

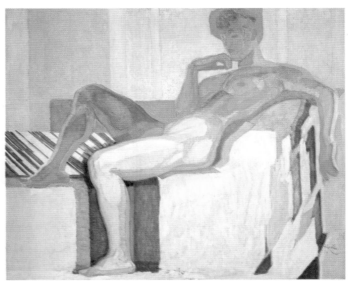

Planes by colours, Large nude, Frank Kupka (1871–1957). Oil on canvas. © Solomon R. Guggenheim Foundation, New York.

Pottery, Patrick Caulfield. Tate Gallery, London.

Photograph by Martin F. Chillmaid.

Support Studies

How we see colours

We see individual colours because an object absorbs some colours and reflects others. For example, a green door is covered with paint which is made to absorb all the rays in white light except green. It reflects these rays back to our eye, so we see only green.

Have you ever wondered why two cans of paint or two pieces of cloth, which seemed to match perfectly in the shop, looked so different when you got them back home? The most probable reason is the lighting.

Colours chosen under artificial light will look very different when seen in natural daylight.

Why does this green door look green?

Fabric photographed in daylight.

Fabric photographed in tungsten light.

Fabric photographed in fluorescent light.

Suggested Assignment

Collect a variety of paint and fabric catalogues by visiting a number of shops. These catalogues will be very useful in many different exercises. They will show the many uses of strong and pale colours.

Who uses colour?

Three groups of people have a great interest in colour. These are the physicist, the psychologist and the artist.

Physicists and colour

Physicists deal with light. The three **primary colours** for the physicist are red, blue and green. These are the primary colours used on the TV screen and in colour photography. They are *not* the primary colours used by the visual artist.

The word primary means 'first'. When two primary colours are mixed together, the result is a **secondary colour**.

The primary and secondary colours of light

Primary colours = red, blue, green
Secondary colours = yellow, cyan, magenta

red + cyan = white light
magenta + green = white light
yellow + blue = white light

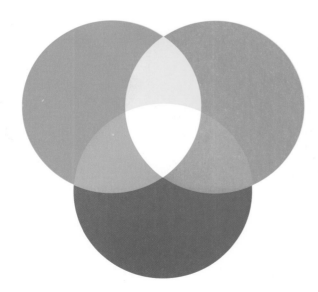

Anyone involved in designing the lighting for theatrical productions will have to know these basic combinations.

Psychologists and colour

Psychologists deal with human response to colour. For example, they know that red can have a stimulating effect, while black can have a depressing effect.

Colour consultants in fashion and beauty put the psychologist's work to good use by emphasising the importance of colour in our overall appearance. They tell us that colour can be the key to looking and feeling our best.

Advertisers use this language of colour in very skilful ways to sell their products.

Observe and Discuss

What is your response to these two roses?

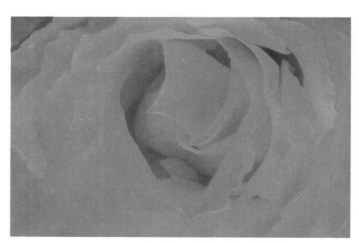

Support Studies

Images dominated by colour

Observe and Discuss

Suggested Assignment

. . . the use of colour in these images and those on page 24.

Collect examples of images which specifically use colour.

Artists and colour

Creative visual artists deal with our response to colour too, but they make use of this information in a different way. Artists may be compared with chemists because they actually mix colour pigments.

The artist's primary colours are red, yellow and blue. This is because he/she is dealing with pigments, not light.

An artist's secondary colours are orange, green and purple.

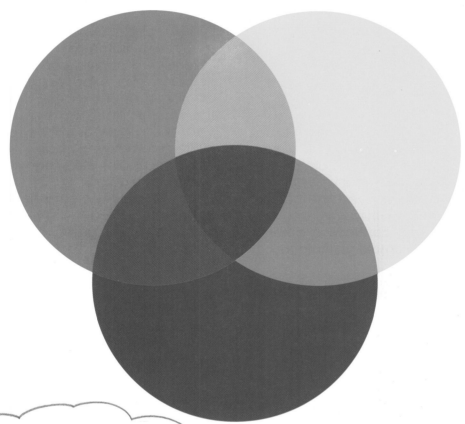

> **Primary colours** = red, yellow, blue
> **Secondary colours** = orange, green, purple
>
> red + yellow = orange
> red + blue = purple
> blue + yellow = green
>
> **Complementary pairs**
> red + green = neutral brown
> yellow + purple = neutral brown
> orange + blue = neutral brown

Suggested Assignments

Use torn or cut tissue paper to make a colour chart of your own.

If you do not have tissue paper, then draw three overlapping circles. Colour them in using either coloured pencils or markers.

There are other colour assignments on page 26.

Support Studies

Complementary colours

The word **complementary** is used for colours, objects or shapes that go well together. Each primary colour has a complementary colour which is produced by mixing the other two primaries. So the complementary colour of blue is orange — a mixture of red and yellow. The complementary colour of red is green — a mixture of yellow and blue. The complementary colour of yellow is purple — a mixture of red and blue.

Contrasting colours

The word **contrast** is used when describing the vast differences between two things — black and white, hot and cold, happy and sad. Contrast also refers to colours which are directly opposite each other on the colour wheel.

All colours that look attractive together are said to complement each other. One of these groups of colours is called **contrasting colours**. Another group is called **harmonious colours**.

Signpost

See harmonious colours, pages 32-34.

Contrasting colours are useful when doing interior decorating. If used in small quantities, they can bring life to a room.

If the eye looks at a colour for any length of time, then the eye needs the soothing effect of the complementary colour.

Suggested Assignments

1. Draw a circle. Divide it into six equal parts. Try mixing some primary and secondary colours and applying an even coat of colour. You can also experience the limitations of different sizes of brushes. Large brushes will be too big for painting a small colour wheel. Hard bristle brushes will be too awkward and stiff to give an even coat.
2. Draw and paint a 12-segment colour wheel. Name each colour.
3. Draw 3 different colour wheels, each showing a primary colour with its complementary opposite — red, green; blue, orange; purple, yellow.

A room plan using complementary colours.

A room plan using contrasting colours.

Support Studies

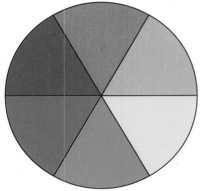

A six-segment colour wheel showing primary and secondary colours.

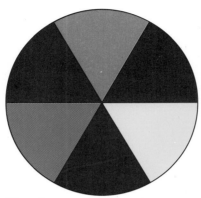

The three primary colours are red, yellow and blue.

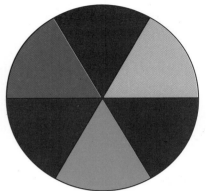

The three secondary colours are orange, green and purple. Each secondary colour is a mixture of two primaries.

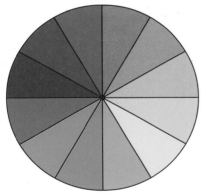

Example of 12-segment colour wheel.

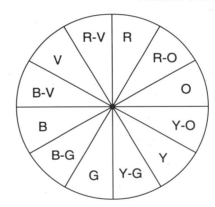

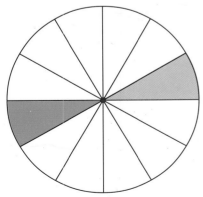

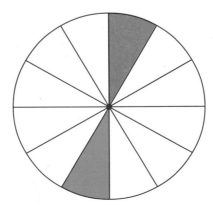

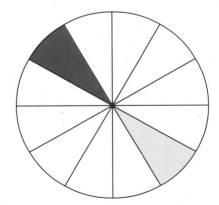

Complementary colours are colours which are directly opposite each other on the colour wheel. The simplest three to remember are red and green, orange and blue, yellow and purple.

Support Studies

SHADES   TINTS

A SHADE is a colour as it moves towards black.   A TINT is a colour as it moves towards white.

TONE - relates to the lightness and or darkness of a colour (regardless of its hue) in a scale from black to white.

HUE - a hue is the strength of a colour as it strikes the eye eg. the redness of the red or the orangeness of the orange etc.

Support Studies

Mixing pairs of complementary colours

If the following pairs of complementary colours (red + green, orange + blue, yellow + purple) are mixed with each other, this will be the result.

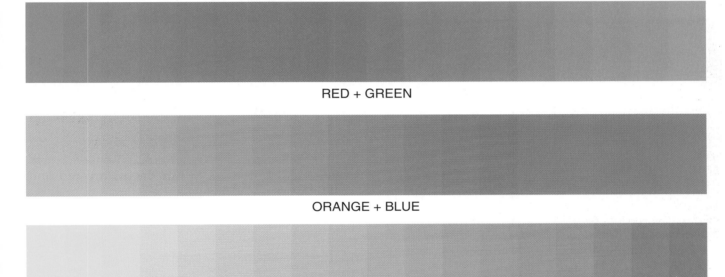

RED + GREEN

ORANGE + BLUE

YELLOW + PURPLE

Suggested Assignments

1. Tint and shade exercise

Measure and rule a page to any size that you wish. You may simply measure one strip if you want to experience the tints and shades of one colour.

Paint your pure colour in the centre box, marked X. Then, add a tiny bit of white to this colour in your mixing well. Paint this new colour in the box to the right of the pure colour. Keep making lighter and lighter tints until you have completed all the boxes to the right.

Now start with your original pure colour again, but this time, add black each time to create shades.

Signpost

Study the Tint and Shade chart, page 28.

2. Tone exercise

The simplest way to paint your tone exercise is to work from white to black.

3. Complementary pairs of colours

When you mix any pair of these complementary colours together (red + green, orange + blue, yellow + purple), you will get browns, or **neutrals**, as they are called.

Support Studies

Examples of contrasting colours in nature

The contrasting colours in this cactus are red and green.

The contrasting colours in this sunset are orange and blue.

The contrasting colours in the autumn trees are rust and green.

The contrasting colours in these lupins are purple and yellow.

Support Studies

Artists' use of contrasting colours

The Merry-go-round, Mark Gertler (1891–1939). Tate Gallery, London.

Marilyn, Andy Warhol (1931–1987). Screen print. Tate Gallery, London.

A first-year student's use of contrasting colours.

La Ferme de Lézavier, Finistère, Roderic O'Conor (1860–1940). Oil on canvas. National Gallery of Ireland.

Support Studies

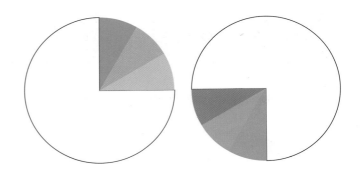

Harmonious colours

Harmonious colours are those which work well together. They are usually found next to each other on the colour wheel.

A good example of colour harmony.

Support Studies

Artists' use of harmonious colours

Cathedral at Rouen, Claude Monet (1840–1926).
Oil on canvas. National Museum, Paris.

The Tholsel, Kilkenny, Paul Henry (1876–1958).
The Butler Gallery, Kilkenny.

Support Studies

Colour harmony in nature

Observe and Discuss

Look at videos, slides or film strips which show how birds and animals blend harmoniously with their backgrounds. Pheasants, snakes, thrushes, crocodiles — indeed many creatures — are great examples of camouflage.

Support Studies

Warm and Cool Colours

- **Warm colours** are those we associate with the sun and fire. They are reds, yellows and oranges.
- **Cool colours** are those we associate with the sea and cold, chilly weather. They are blues, greens and purples.

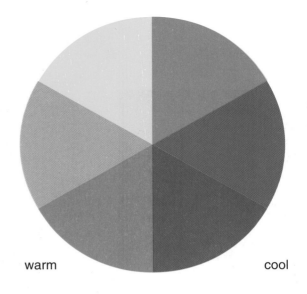

warm   cool

Warm colours in nature.

Cool colours in nature.

Combinations of warm and cool colours in patchwork, designed and made by Maureen Roche.

Suggested Assignments

1. Draw or paint a colour wheel showing the warm and cool colours.
2. Collect pictorial examples that show:
   (a) warm colours only; (b) cool colours only.

Support Studies

Colour intensity

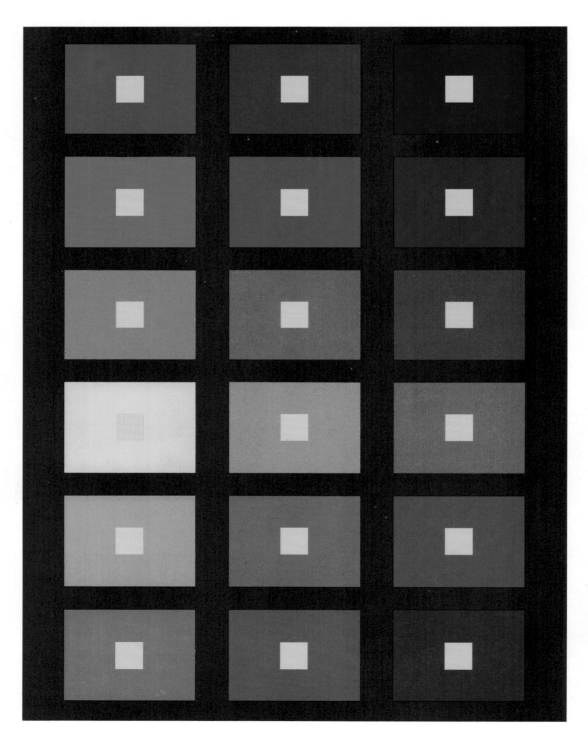

Support Studies

Colour intensity

Any colour can be made more intense by placing it against a different background. When a neutral grey is placed next to any other colour, the grey veers towards the complement of that colour. The edges of light colours bleed, so that they appear to be larger. But darker tones appear to look smaller because of their sharp edges.

Colour illusion

Colour loses its intensity as it recedes into the atmosphere. The colour of grass is constant — green. But hills in the distance can appear blue. Yellow in the distance will look white. Yet we all know that grass is not blue because we are able to distinguish between illusion and fact.

Note how both the greens and blues become less intense in the distance.

Signpost

See Local colour, page 40.

Direction of natural light

Northern light is rich in blue rays. Southern light is rich in yellow rays. This can be shown by these two photographs at the right.

This point is very important when it comes to home decorating. Rooms that face north need to be given some warm colours to make them feel cosy. Rooms that face south can still be friendly even when cool colours are used.

Rooms

Small rooms such as hallways or very boxy bedrooms will look larger if they are painted in pastel colours, or even lighter tones of these colours.

Big rooms often appear bare and cold. Warm colours and tones of red, yellow and orange appear to bring the room surfaces closer together. In large rooms, their use will help to bring in walls and lower ceilings. Darker shades of all other colours have a similar effect.

High ceilings can be 'lowered' by painting them in darker tones than the walls. Low ceilings can look 'higher' by painting them a lighter tone than the wall. Narrow rooms such as long, dark hallways will benefit dramatically if they are painted in light colours.

Observe and Discuss

Have you ever experienced any of these colour effects at home or at school?

A vase in northern light...   ...and in southern light.

Support Studies

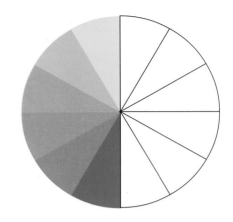

Choosing four colour schemes based on the colour wheel

Warm colours

Red, orange and yellow are **warm colours**. They are associated with hot, sunny days and cosy winter fires. Warm colours will brighten up a sunless room. Remember that red, orange and yellow are very strong in their natural states. They are very dominant and will be much more effective if used as accent colours. Tints of these colours — pinks, salmons, peaches and soft yellows — are more versatile to use. Since they are warm and cheerful, they are especially good living room colours.

Cool colours

Because we associate green, blue and purple with the sea, we refer to them as **cool colours**. They are used to create a cool, calm atmosphere.

Here we see a variety of blues being used. As cool colours recede into the distance, they will make a small room look larger. Never use them in dark rooms which face north, as they will make the room appear even colder.

Warm, sunny rooms cope well with cool colour schemes without appearing cold.

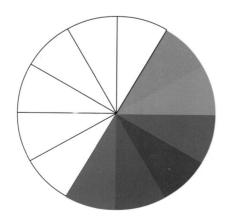

Support Studies

Contrasting colours

Contrasting colours (red\green, orange\blue, yellow\purple) are found opposite each other on the colour wheel. They can be used together to brighten up a room. These pairs of colours are sometimes referred to as **complementary colours**. They intensify each other when placed together.

Signpost

Refer to the colour wheel on page 25 for more details.

In this room, contrasting colours of red and green, blue and yellow have been used. White is used to give a bright feeling to the room.

Contrasting colours should not be used in equal amounts. One colour should dominate. Here, the yellow armchair dominates and links the whole room together.

Harmonious colours

Any group of three or four colours that lie next to each other on the colour wheel are said to be **harmonious**. This is because these colours are closely related.

Signpost

Look at the colour wheels on page 27 for a variety of examples.

In this example, a blue tone of green, a green tone of blue and a blue have been combined in the overall colour scheme. Because none of the colours is dominant, they work well together.

An orangey-red colour has been introduced in the fabric of the armchair. This is a contrasting colour to the blue-greens and helps to add a warm touch to the scheme. The addition of a small amount of contrasting colours to any harmonious scheme will give it life and make it more interesting.

Contrasting colours will always complement each other. Complementary colours can be either contrasting or harmonious, depending on the colours used.

Support Studies

Colour symbolism and meaning

Many **symbols** are used in human communication. For example, the cross is a symbol of Christianity, while the dove is a symbol of peace. A ring symbolises love that never ends. White is a symbol of purity, while red signifies danger.

How colour is used

Colour is used in three ways — personal, local and symbolic.

- The **personal use of colour** is not bound by any rules, as these interpretations of a cone show. Each person's use of colour is completely different and very personal.

The same pine cone as interpreted by three different students.

- **Local colour** refers to the colours in the scene being viewed. If this is a landscape or a seascape, one must remember that the atmosphere will affect how we see the colour. Distant colours will always be softer and less intense.

- **Symbolic colours** get their meanings from various civilisations of the world. From these, colour-coded systems have evolved that are accepted worldwide. A few examples of this include the colours of traffic lights, the colours used in electric wiring and the colours of national flags.

Find out about the colour symbolism in the Irish flag.

Do brides wear white in all countries?

Suggested Assignment

Collect examples of colour symbolism – - flags, wiring systems, traffic lights etc. — as they are recognised throughout the world.

Signpost

See colour illusion, page 37.

Support Studies

The association of colours with emotion

We use red in a wide number of ways to show various emotions or conditions.

red-faced	→	embarrassed
seeing red	→	very angry
in the red	→	in debt
painting the town red	→	having a great time
red-handed	→	guilty
red hot	→	intense heat
red-blooded	→	virile

Blue and green are also associated with emotions.
- He left town under a blue cloud.
- blue with the cold
- once in a blue moon
- out of the blue
- green with envy

Suggested Assignment

Lists like these can be gathered under many colour headings. Try it and see!

Observe and Discuss

What types of symbolic colours are used today in advertisements?

Different colour associations

What colour do we associate with mourning and funerals? In western society, we would say black. But in India, the answer would be white. Violet is used in Turkey and yellow in Burma.

The colour associated with royalty also varies, depending on the country. We associate purple with royalty; it dates back to the ancient Egyptians. In China, however, the royal colour was yellow, while in ancient Rome it was red.

In the west, we associate white with bridal wear. But in China, the traditional bridal colour is red, while in Hindu India, the choice is yellow.

Symbolic colours are less important in art today than they once were. But artists still use them to add impact to their statements.

What colour is used in this funeral in Bali?

41

Support Studies

Symbolism and meaning from around the world

Weavers in Scotland give their woollen fabrics distinctive bands of colours. These fabrics are known as **tartans**. Each tartan shows the colours of a particular family or clan. As families intermarried and moved to different areas, the tartans became more and more complicated. For example, the background colour of one clan's tartan might be divided by a couple of lines of colour from another clan. This has led to very complex tartans. These tartans provide one of the world's simplest but most effective systems of heraldry.

Traditional Indian dyes and dyeing techniques vary greatly from region to region. Simply by looking at a woman's sari, an expert can tell from which part of the sub-continent she comes.

Traditional dyeing methods extract colours from native plants and insects. These colours are as bright and vibrant as any synthetic dyes. The peacock blues and shocking pinks are as distinctly Indian as are the rich earth reds and saffron yellows.

Black and White

Let's conclude this chapter by dealing with black and white — the most powerful contrasts.

According to some, black and white are not even colours. But the very fact that they exist as pigments can be used as an argument to include them as artist's colours.

Only black and white insist on purity. Add the slightest tinge of any other colour and they lose their intensity. Nothing can be lighter than white or darker than black.

Black and white are **extremes of tone**.

In Scotland tartans are still worn on special occasions. The main picture shows a traditional Scottish piper wearing a tartan kilt, along with close-up views of tartans.

Pattern and Shape

Random autumnal leaf pattern by 13-14 year old students.

Geometric pattern on a Greek cup, showing a horse race and a funeral procession. National Museum, Athens.

Patterned silk at an Indian market.

Patterned gift wrap.

Support Studies

Pattern is an indispensable part of our daily lives. From the earliest times, humans have used patterns to beautify their bodies, their homes, their weapons, utensils and other possessions.

The use of pattern probably dates back even further than the Egyptians in the Nile Valley. Because of their desire to improve their environment, the Egyptians painted patterns on all their possessions. In the same way, tribes from all over the world use patterns for ceremonial body paintings, for jewellery, bark paintings and tree carvings.

The Surma people of Ethiopia use chalk, water and ochre to decorate their bodies. The patterns on this warrior are meant to intimidate his enemies.

Signpost

See face painting, page 123.

This pattern of geese was painted on the wall of an Egyptian tomb in about 1400 BC.

The Masai people are nomadic. Because of this they have developed an elaborate and decorative style of beadwork which focuses on their bodies. The colours and patterns tell about such things as the family, its wealth and possessions.

The Masai people of Kenya wear elaborate jewellery.

Support Studies

Native Americans express themselves through body painting, clothing, elaborate beadwork, quill stitching on animal skins and many other artefacts. They use geometrical patterns in their woven blankets and rugs. Designs and patterns reflect their feelings about their experiences and their environment.

Navaho rugs were originally woven in dyed wool with plain indigo stripes. The patterns were copied from the Hopi and Zuni tribes. By the end of the nineteenth century, Navaho rugmakers were using stronger patterns and colours.

This pair of leather moccasins was made by the Plains Indians and decorated with beads and porcupine quills.

A Navaho rug with geometric patterns is being woven on a hand loom.

A shirt for a Plains Indian decorated with porcupine quills. The round pattern at the top represents bullets. This is believed to give protection against enemy weapons.

Support Studies

What is a pattern? What is a shape?

• **A pattern is created when a group of related shapes, lines or marks is united together.**

• **A shape is any area enclosed by a line**.

A shape can be **abstract** — it does not have to look like an identifiable object. Shapes can be made to look more interesting by adding colour and texture.

The word **relationship** means that different things are connected in some way. For a relationship to exist, people or objects must have something in common. The first relationship that we experienced was within the family. In a landscape, a group of fields will form a pattern on the horizon because they are related or connected to each other.

Patterns can be **natural, manmade** or **applied**.

Natural patterns

If we look at a tree, we will notice that the leaves form different patterns. Each tree has its own pattern of leaves. These distinctive patterns help us to recognise different species of trees. The pattern of leaves will also depend on the angle from which the tree is viewed.

In this natural pattern of beech leaves, some of the shapes overlap. These create darker patches of colour where the light does not shine through. These dark patches make a pattern of their own.

In this bunch of flowers, there are three patterns — the light patches, the dark patches (shadows) and the vibrant orange centres.

Support Studies

Natural patterns

Clouds form patterns in the sky.

Trees create patterns.

A pattern of leaves.

Birds like this sparrowhawk have patterned feathers.

Stones can form patterns.

A pattern of geese.

Observe and Discuss

Suggested Assignment

Talk about these natural patterns. Observe light and dark, different colours and tones, and any other features of the patterns which you and your class find interesting.

Collect a wide variety of pictures of natural patterns. Arrange them in groups — like flowers, stones, birds etc.

Support Studies

Manmade patterns

Brick pattern.

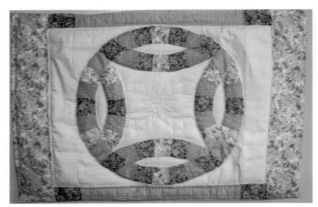

A patchwork pattern.

A Turkish woman weaves an elaborately patterned carpet.

Stonework pattern.

Field pattern.

The pattern of windows in the American Embassy, Dublin.

Observe and Discuss

. . .the manmade patterns shown in these photographs.

Support Studies

Applied pattern is used solely for decoration. The decoration is applied to a surface. It has no function in itself.

Applied pattern

Support Studies

How to make a pattern

To make a pattern, the shapes must be unified. This unity makes the shapes look like they belong together. We might also use the word 'harmony' when speaking about pattern. We looked at colour harmony in the last chapter. On page 44 we saw how the Masai tribespeople use special forms of unity to tell their life stories in their beadwork.

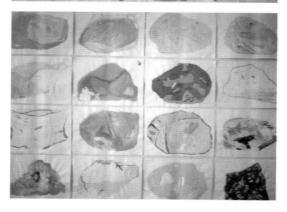

The illustrations (below left) show a number of paintings of snail shells, pine cones and stones by first-year students. These paintings have been combined to form interesting patterns. First, the subject of each picture is taken from the same family of shapes. Secondly, the pattern is made by placing the pictures next to each other in a group. All of the pictures in the group touch each other.

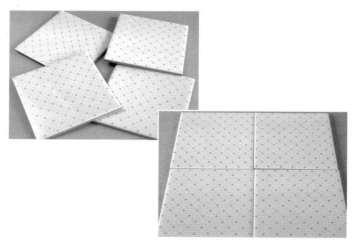

In the same way, patterns are made using wall tiles. If the various tiles are separated from each other, or if they are unrelated, a pattern will not exist because there is no unity between the tiles.

In a pattern, you must first see the whole picture before you see the individual parts or shapes.

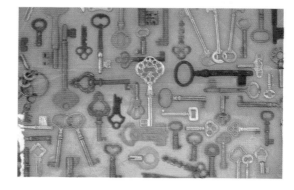

This picture shows a pattern of keys. All the keys are different in size and shape, but they all belong to one family — keys. They form a pattern because they have been carefully arranged, making the best use of the space around each key or bunch of keys.

How to create unity

1. Putting the shapes close together

In Example A, the leaves are floating on the page. They have no special relationship with each other.

In Example B, the shapes are placed close together, making them look pleasing to the eye.

| Example A | Example B |

2. Repetition

When making manmade applied patterns, repetition is the most widely used device for creating unity.

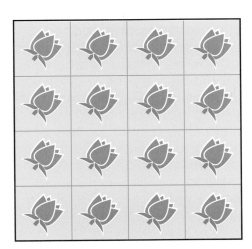

3. Continuation

Continuation means that something continues, whether it is a shape or a line, from one area to the other. This helps lead the eye from one area to the next. Artists often use this method to create harmony within a picture. Graphic designers use it when planning layouts for books, magazines, advertisements etc.

A good example of continuation—the field of wild flowers wraps around the front, spine and back of this book jacket.

4. Unity with variety

It is possible to make a pattern so united that it becomes boring to look at. The artist's aim is to add interest to this pattern by introducing some variety. This can be achieved by varying the colours or shapes, or by introducing lines into each box. Variety is necessary in all forms of patterns.

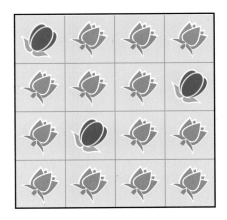

A geometric pattern showing a great sense of variety.

Bees at a honeycomb (humans aren't the only creatures that make patterns!).

Suggested Assignments

1. Collect samples of patterns of:
   (a) natural patterns — honeycombs, butterflies, flowers, foliage, feathers etc.
   (b) manmade patterns — brickwork, slates, buildings, architectural ornaments etc.
   (c) applied patterns from (a) and (b), used in fabric, wallpaper, pottery etc.
2. Research and collect patterns from one or more of these styles:
   (a) Egyptian
   (b) Renaissance
   (c) Celtic
   (d) Art Nouveau

Grids

Grids are measured guidelines which a designer uses when creating a pattern. Care must be taken when measuring a grid, since any inaccuracies can spoil the pattern.

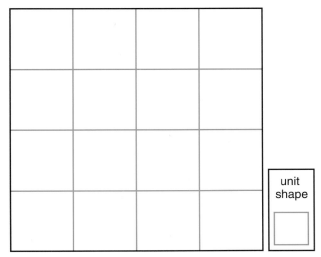

1. Square grid.

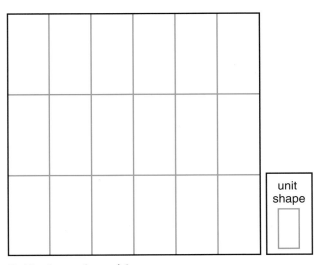

2. Rectangular grid.

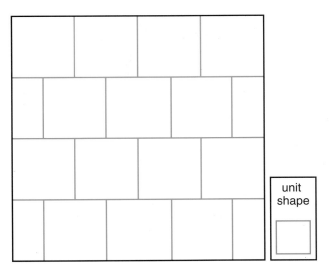

3. Side-drop square grid.

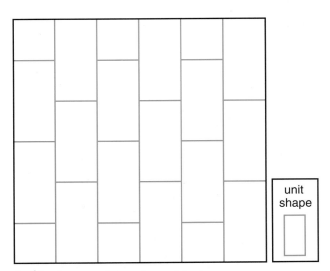

4. $^1/_2$ drop rectangular grid.

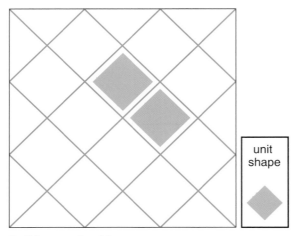

unit shape

5. Diamond grid.

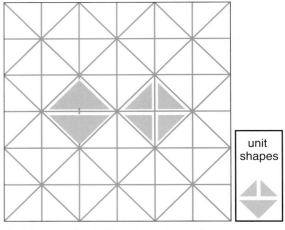

unit shapes

8. Diamond grid broken down into either 2 triangles or 4 triangles.

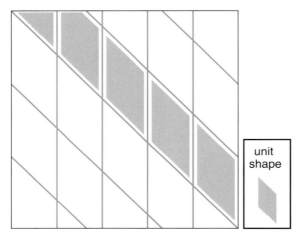

unit shape

6. Parallelogram grid.

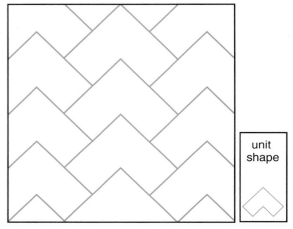

unit shape

9. L-shaped grid on side.

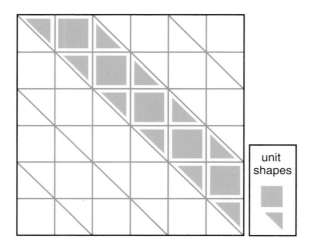

unit shapes

7. Square and triangle grid.

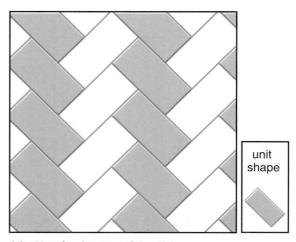

unit shape

10. Herringbone grid, all boxes identical in size.

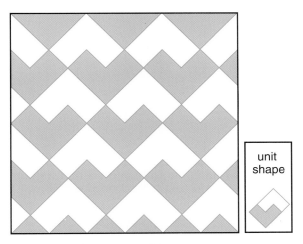

11. Variations on L grid.

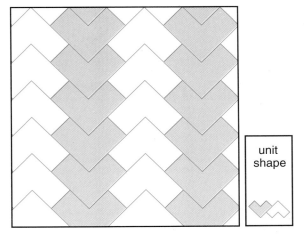

12. Variations on L grid.

Different grids with different patterns

A **motif** is that part of a pattern which is repeated. The patterns shown here are all self-explanatory, except for the linking pattern, which is dealt with separately on page 58.

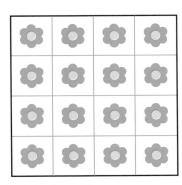

1. Isolated motif on a square grid.

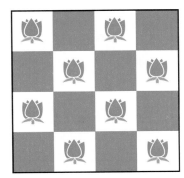

2. Every second section a motif, every second section blank (isolated) on a square grid.

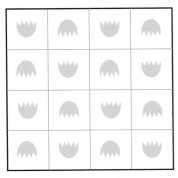

3. Every second section change direction of motif on a square grid.

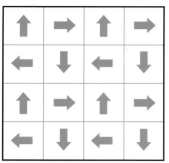

4. Change motif every 4 sections (isolated) on a square grid.

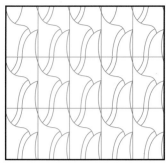

8. Linking pattern on a rectangular grid (explained on page 58).

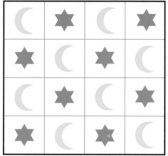

5. Put a different motif in every second section (isolated) on a square grid.

9. Reverse (negative/positive) motif on a square grid.

6. Let motif touch the sides (non isolated) on a square grid.

10. Diamond (isolated) motif on a diamond grid.

7. Inverted flick-over pattern using a square grid.

11. Isolated single motif on a half-drop square grid.

12. Isolated motif on a pointed arrow grid.

13. Diagonal line pattern (steady design).

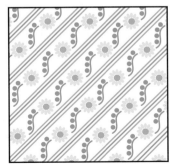

14. Diagonal line and drop design.

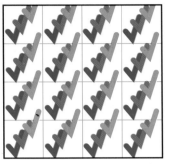

15. Overlapping repeat motif on a rectangular grid.

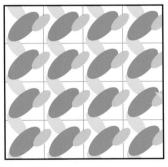

16. Overlapping different motifs on a square grid.

Overlapping motifs can be very effective if done in harmonious colours.

Signposts

See colour harmony, page 32.

How to make a linking pattern

1. Start with a half-drop grid 2 x 3 or 2 x 4. (A half-drop looks like a brick wall on its side.)
2. Then draw a line in each section of the grid. Tracing paper may be used for greater accuracy.
3. Then draw another line. With a third line, you can rub out your grid and continue on adding lines for colour and/or texture.
4. Be careful not to draw your lines into corners as this will spoil the pattern.

This method of linking-up patterns may be done with other grids. But the half-drop is the best one.

The 'linking' pattern is probably the most effective, if done correctly. (It is better to have a simpler pattern done correctly than to attempt a complicated one and do it badly.)

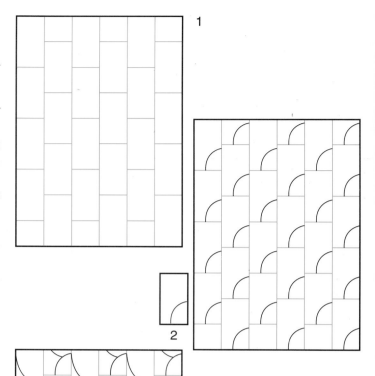

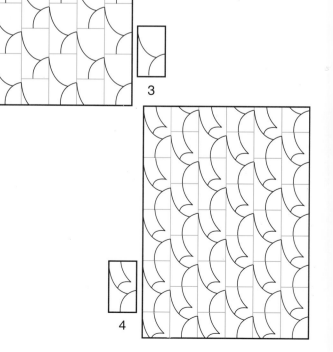

Colour suggestions

Until you can control your colours, here are some suggested combinations of colour for patterns.

Primaries	Complementaries	Harmonious
blue + red	red + green	red + purple
blue + yellow	yellow + purple	red + orange
red + yellow	blue + orange	blue + green
		blue + purple
		yellow + orange
		yellow + green

Tints and shades of grey and beige may be used with these colour combinations.

Do not use black for the moment. It is too hard to control. Leave plenty of white.

THEMES	RECOGNISABLE MOTIF	SUGGESTED (SYMBOLIC)
Christmas	Holly leaf	Abstract holly leaf
Easter	Easter egg	Suggestion of broken egg
Autumn	Leaf	Leaf shape
Valentine	Heart	Abstract of half-heart shape
Baby	Rattle	Pattern on rattle

Cloud shape abstract in itself

Suggested Assignment

Try out linking patterns using the combinations of colours, shapes and motifs shown in the book.

Students' Pattern Work

First-year students' first attempts at all-over patterns, using coloured pencils and a mixture of grids and styles.

Third-year students' linking patterns, made with tracing paper.

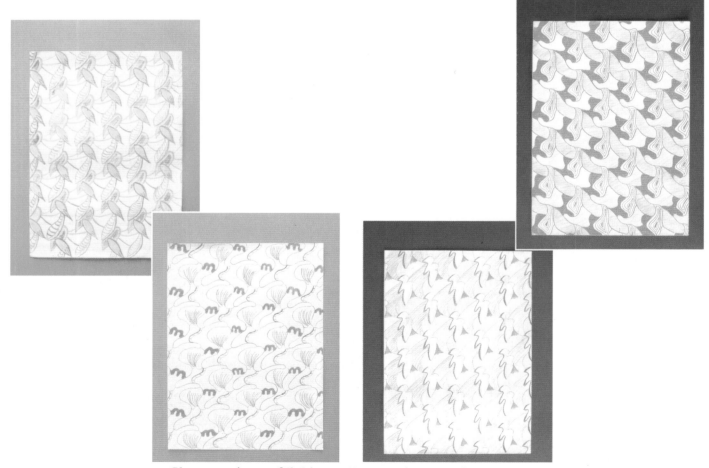

Close-up views of linking patterns using a half-drop grid.

Students' Pattern Work (12-16 years)

with Themes, Peparatory Work and Support Studies

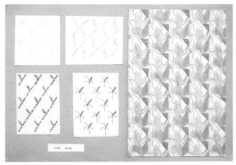

Students' development of a linking pattern and half-drop grids, together with some preparatory studies.

The eye as a Theme, built into a linking pattern, with Support Studies

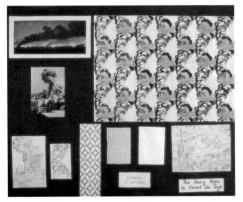

War Theme (tank). Linking pattern with Support Studies and preparatory work. Open pattern with half-drop grid.

Kitchen Theme (iron) showing close-up of iron repeated into a linking pattern with half-drop grid.

War Theme (explosion) pattern, with preparatory work and Support Studies. Half-drop grid.

Hair Theme (curl) with preparatory work and Support Studies. Half-drop grid.

Flower Theme, square/diamond grid, showing a variety of possibilities with Support Studies.

Support Studies

Art Deco

The term **Art Deco** comes from the Paris exhibition of 1925. Art Deco soon came to influence artists and printmakers, as well as furniture designers. They saw it as a colourful and exciting modern style. Its use continued throughout the 1930s, using rather heavy, geometric simplification of form. Its patterns were bold and very decorative.

The examples of giftwrapping paper on pages 62 and 63 were taken from the colourful book, *Kaleidoscope,* published in 1925. They all show different forms of abstract geometric Art Deco patterns.

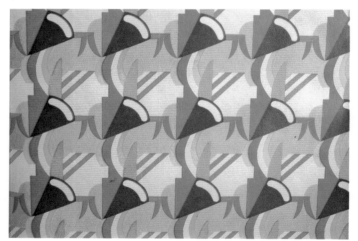

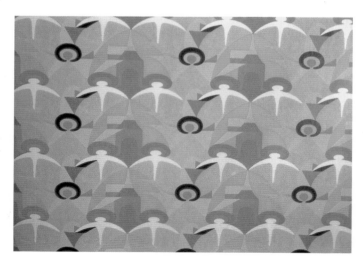

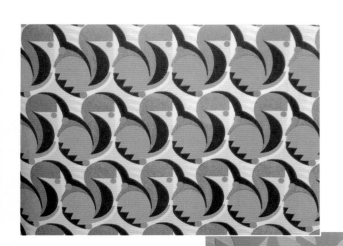

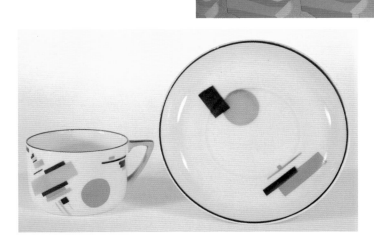

Observe and Discuss

What is your reaction to these Art Deco patterns and objects?
Discuss why you like or dislike this style.

Support Studies

William Morris

William Morris (1834–96) began to design fabrics and wallpapers in the 1860s. He was influenced by Gothic patterns and he admired medieval craftspeople who not only designed but printed their own work.

Nature had a strong influence in Morris' work. Many of his patterns came from medieval and Indian textiles. He returned to traditional dye-stuffs and the wood-block method of printing. Morris was a superb printmaker. His patterns greatly influenced the **Art Nouveau** style which developed in the 1890s.

Willow Boughs, a William Morris design from 1887. The rhythm of the sweeping leaves shows Morris' ability and skill at concealing a repeat pattern. The 'Sussex' chair in the foreground was designed by Morris' colleague, Phillip Webb.

Evenlode is an 1883 design which Morris named after a tributary of the River Thames.

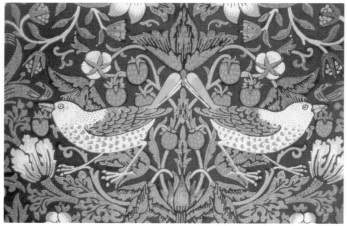

Strawberry Thief, 1883, by William Morris. This small bird pattern is derived from a fifteenth-century Italian silk design, but it still has Morris' own unique quality.

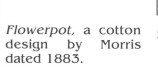

Flowerpot, a cotton design by Morris dated 1883.

Signpost

See Art Nouveau, pages 74-77.

Support Studies

Manmade lines

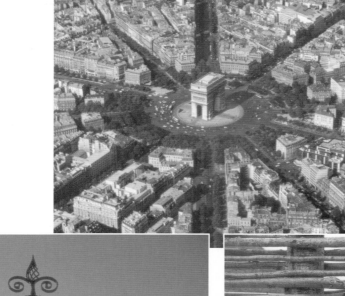

Support Studies

Applied lines

A line pattern for wrapping paper.

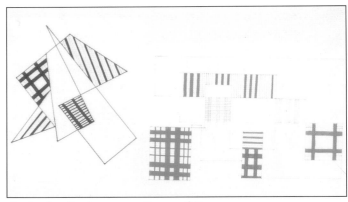

A student's drawn pattern of lines.

Wrapping paper often uses bold lines.

This Art Nouveau pattern by René Beauclair uses sinuous and graceful lines.

What is line?

Of all of the elements in art, **line** is probably the one that we are most familiar with. Because most of our drawing and writing tools are pointed, we have been making lines since we were very small children.

What is a line? A line can be a path traced by a moving point or dot. It can be as simple as a mark made by a pointed tool. A line is created by movement. So every line is said to have thickness, direction and rhythm.

- **Thickness** —The width of a line or mark.
- **Direction** —The forward movement of the line.
- **Rhythm** —A sense of movement. It can be created by regular or irregular lines, or by marks made by different tools.

Line has a great ability to suggest things to us. So it can convey all sorts of moods and feelings.

Lines divide the surface of a picture into a variety of shapes. The shapes are created by lines which may be long and narrow, tall and thin, straight or curved.

Hard lines.

Soft and gentle lines.

Angry lines.

Dancing lines.

Our surroundings have a **linear** quality. This can be either horizontal or vertical.

Horizontal means straight across, parallel to the horizon.

Vertical means straight up and down.

Humans are basically vertical beings. We live in a world full of vertical lines — houses, lampposts, telephone poles, trees, pipes etc.

A pine forest gives us a great sense of movement and restlessness. This is due to the vertical nature of the trees.

By contrast, the horizontal lines of a seascape or landscape give us a sense of peacefulness and restfulness.

Diagonal lines suggest motion.

The Gothic architecture in Canterbury Cathedral (above) and in Salisbury Cathedral (below) features strong vertical lines.

If the lines in a picture are mostly horizontal and the **format** (layout) is also horizontal, then the feelings that we experience are quiet, calm and peaceful. If the format of the same picture changes from horizontal to vertical, the effect also changes.

Here are two examples of this effect. The first format has been changed from vertical to horizontal. The second example has changed from a horizontal format to a vertical format.

Observe and Discuss

. . . the effects of the changes in format in these photographs.

71

All lines have energy, although some lines are more powerful than others. Lines in some plants are definite and strong, while those in a weeping willow are weak and drooping.

Natural lines such as those found in trees and plants have a soothing effect on us. Because of this, it is important to plant trees and shrubs around buildings. This helps to soften these hard-edged structures. It is also important to have plants inside our buildings, where they give the same calming effect.

Line is important because it can describe shape. It is by shape that we recognise objects. The drawing below is immediately understood as a picture of a hand. It does not have the width or thickness of a real hand. Nor does it have the same colour and texture. It is not the actual size of a hand. Yet we recognise it because of its distinctive outline and shape.

Line is therefore very important. With a few short strokes, the artist can create shapes which we can understand and recognise.

Signpost

See page 132 for drawings of hands.

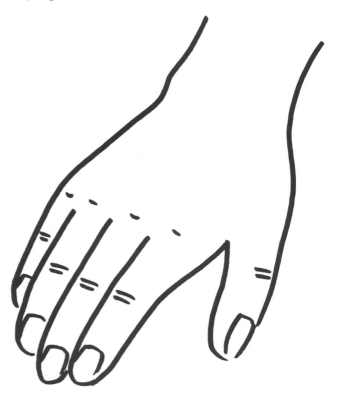

Suggested Assignments

Collect examples of linear patterns from:
- The natural environment
- The manmade environment
- Applied lines

Support Studies

Line in art movements

The entrance stone at Newgrange.

The linear art of Newgrange

One of the earliest examples of line carved on stone can still be seen on the entrance stone at Newgrange, Co. Meath (above). It is decorated in abstract spirals and geometric patterns. Newgrange dates from the Neolithic (New Stone Age) period — about 2500 BC.

Celtic Art

One of the earliest art movements to make excellent use of line was **Celtic La Tène** art. The Celts were a group of people who reached Ireland around 200 BC, where they introduced their La Tène culture. The name La Tène comes from a site in Switzerland which was an early centre of Celtic civilisation.

Celtic designs were mainly based on the circle. Sometimes, however, spirals and other geometric patterns were used.

The Turoe Stone in Co. Galway is one of the finest examples of Celtic stone carving. The stone is covered with continuous loops and curves. These carry the eye in a full circle around the stone.

The Celts did not only work on stone. Look at the Broighter Collar (below). It is a fine example of the Celtic skills at metalwork. The collar is a gold torc which was probably made between 75 BC and the first century AD. It is decorated in flowing curves using a **repoussé** technique. Repoussé means beaten out from behind. The collar also has a very intricate locking device.

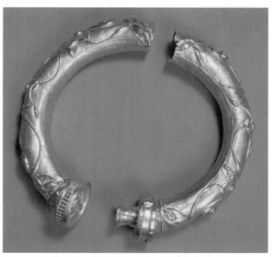

The Broighter Collar (c.75 BC). National Museum of Ireland.

Support Studies

Art Nouveau

The term **Art Nouveau** comes from a shop in Paris called 'L'Art Nouveau' which was opened in 1895. The shop displayed a variety of luxury items by English, Belgian, American and French designers.

Art Nouveau can be described as a style in art which uses clean, flowing lines and swirling, asymetrical compositions. These compositions are based on beautiful female figures using exaggerated floral and natural forms.

The Art Nouveau style began in the 1890s and continued into the early years of the twentieth century. It was applied to a wide range of objects — wallpaper, textiles, ceramics, embroidery, stained glass, furniture and architecture.

The first object to use the sinuous lines of Art Nouveau was probably a chair made between 1882–83 by the English designer, Arthur H. Mackmurdo. The textile and wallpaper designs produced by the Arts and Crafts Movement in England in the 1880s were the influence behind the Continental Art Nouveau of the 1890s. European design, especially in France, was influenced by Japanese prints and objects.

One of the first designs to be called Art Nouveau was this chair made in 1882-83 by Arthur H. Mackmurdo.

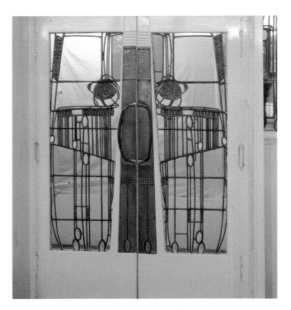

Another Art Nouveau designer, Charles Rennie Macintosh, created these doors for the Willow Tea Room in Glasgow in 1898.

Support Studies

At the turn of the century, the fashion for stained glass was at its height. Stained glass doors, like those shown on page 74, became part of every middle-class house in England's suburbs.

Many other artists were noted for their Art Nouveau style of work. They included Henry Van de Velde, Aubrey Beardsley, Louis Comfort Tiffany, Gustave Klimt, Loetz Witwe and Victor Horta.

Work by Beardsley and other Art Nouveau artists was reproduced in the *Studio* magazine at the time. So it is easy to see how the work of one artist may have influenced the other.

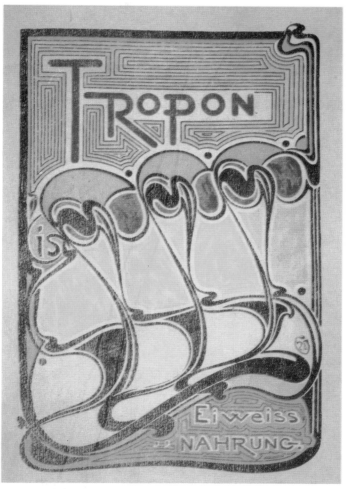

Tropon, a poster designed around 1899 by Henry Van de Velde. Victoria and Albert Museum.

The Peacock Shirt, a book illustration by Aubrey Beardsley (1872–1898). British Museum.

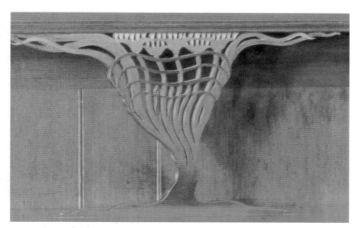

Detail of fretwork brackets from a mahogany cabinet designed around 1885 by Arthur H. Mackmurdo.

Support Studies

More Art Nouveau

A Tiffany lamp with leaded glass and brass featuring a dragonfly motif.

A vase with metalwork, made by Loetz Witwe.

The entrance hall and staircase designed by Victor Horta for his home in Brussels.

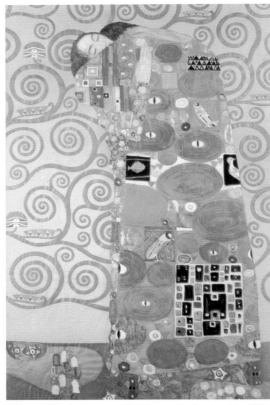

The Embrace, Gustav Klimt (1862--1918). Mixed media with silver and gold leaf on paper. Musée de Strasbourg.

Support Studies

René Beauclair

René Beauclair published pattern books of wrapping paper in the Art Nouveau style around 1900. He used soft pastels in his patterns, making them ideally suited for wallpaper and textiles. Art Nouveau designers had a preference for exotic flowers, and Beauclair was no exception. His patterns, a few of which are shown here, developed from studies of lilies, orchids and passion flowers.

Support Studies

Artists' use of line

The Grey Tree, Piet Mondrian (1872–1944).
Haags Gemeentemuseum, The Netherlands.

Still Life with Goat's Head and Bottle,
Pablo Picasso (1881–1973). Tate
Gallery, London.

Suggested Assignments

1. Experiment with tools for recording lines — brush and ink, pen and ink, felt-tip pens, chalks, crayons, string etc.

Signpost

See Drawing, pages 97-101.

2. Make run-line and blown-line pictures. Look at the examples. Take care not to get dizzy!

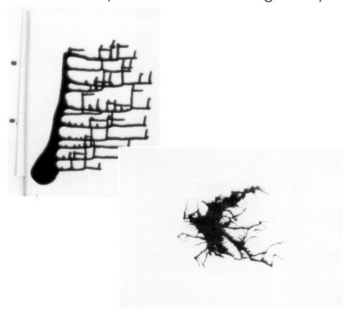

3. Make a finger painting of a tree using water-based paint on a washable surface. Now take a print from it.

Signpost

See Printing, pages 178,185.

4. Collect examples of: (a) lines of different thickness, direction and rhythm; (b) your own examples of how line was used in various art movements or by various artists.

5. String can be very versatile. Using different widths of string, create your own linear pattern. The ones in the illustrations at right are based on the circle.

6. Based on previous drawings and research, create a linear design suitable for block printing, lino printing or string printing.

Signpost

See Lino Printing, page 302.

7. Experiment with line used to indicate tone, cross-hatching etc. Refer to the work of Michelangelo, da Vinci and others.

Signpost

See Drawing, page 101.

8. Make a linear design suitable for a greeting card. Use one colour only.

Texture

Fungi on tree, Rod Tuach.

Support Studies

Texture means surface quality. The texture of something can be rough, as with jagged rocks. Or it can be smooth, as with silk or polished marble.

Look at the texture of this rock face.

To experience texture, we use our sense of touch. Sometimes, we do not actually have to feel the object to experience its texture. Our memories have already stored a variety of touch sensations gathered from birth.

Note the texture of this piece of marble.

Describe the texture of straw.

The texture of an angry sea.

Discuss the texture of feathers and fruit (this is a male blackcap eating an apple).

Natural textures

Natural textures by the beach.

The texture of a waterfall.

Texture on a snowy branch.

Frost has texture.

The texture of a dog's fur.

Natural texture in a cornfield.

Manmade textures

I went to the mountains, Des Dillon (1964 -   ). Woven tapestry. Mixed media—woven fleece, cottons, tweeds, felt. 1.5m x 0.9m (5ft x 3ft).

Corrugated card.

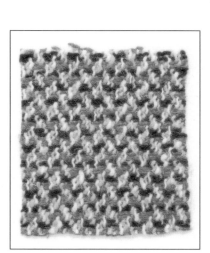

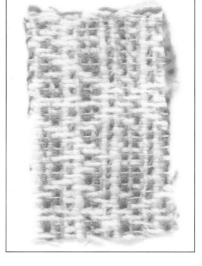

Woven fabric (wool).

The use of texture in sculpture

An Iron Age head, Armagh Cathedral.

Female head, Cashel, Co. Tipperary.

Birds in Flight, John Behan.
Welded bronze.

The Children of Lir, Oisin Kelly.
Garden of Remembrance, Dublin.

Signpost

See 3D, pages 257-282.

Applied texture for decorative purposes

Decorative pottery often has a textured appearance. This plate was made by Michael Kennedy of Sligo Pottery.

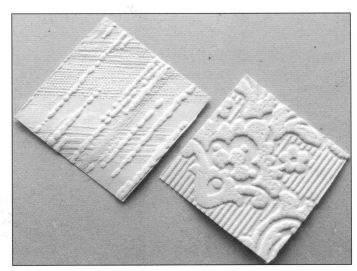

Textured wallpaper.

Textured glass.

A cobblestone street.

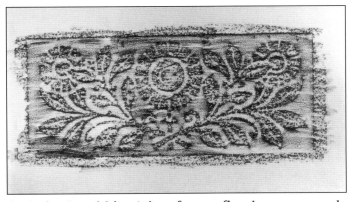

A student's rubbing taken from a fireplace surround.

A garden wall made with Roadstone blocks.

Support Studies

Some **craft materials** are excellent for exploring and achieving textural effects — wool in weaving, various clays in ceramics, metals and stones in jewellery, wood for carving.

Architects are also aware of texture. They put their knowledge to great use by employing contrasting textures in building materials. This makes the building more visually interesting.

Textures suitable for a 'feely board'.

Suggested Assignments

1. Make your own 'feely board'. Use as many textures as possible.
2. Combine your textured objects to make a class 'feely board'.

Rubbings

Almost everyone has done a coin rubbing. It is just as easy to do an art rubbing. Just place a sheet of paper (preferably newsprint) on top of a textured surface. Scribble gently and evenly over the paper with crayon, chalk or a dark pencil.

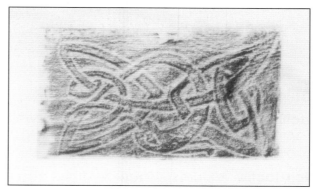

A leather rubbing.

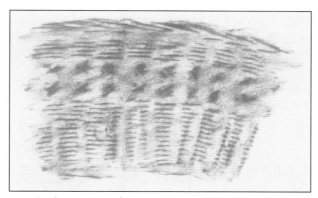

A rubbing taken from a straw basket.

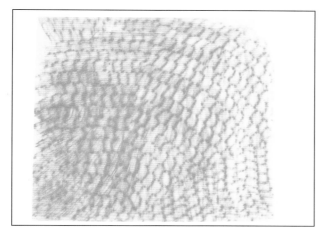

A rubbing taken from a woollen shawl.

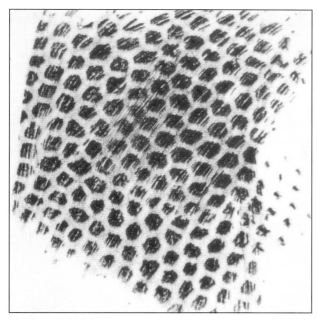

A glass rubbing.

Signpost

See Rubbing, page 85.

Suggested Assignments

1. Make rubbings of as many different types of textures as you can. Use newsprint and rub with crayons, chalk or pencil.
2. Some churches (e.g. St. Canice's in Kilkenny) have old tombs from which you can make rubbings. Find out whether it is possible to take rubbings in a church near you.

Observe and Discuss

Which rubbings were the most/least successful? Talk about what makes a good rubbing.

Support Studies

Tactile and non-tactile textures

- **Tactile textures** — These are textures which can be experienced by touching them. A good example is the bark of a tree.

- **Non-tactile textures**—These textures can be *experienced*, but *not touched*, Many surfaces give the impression of being textured when in fact they are not. Modern lino floor coverings often have a textured appearance when, in fact, they are completely flat.

Dürer, Van Eyck and Vermeer show us a variety of textures in their work when in fact the surface of each painting is flat. This type of texture is **non-tactile**.

Suggested Assignment

Find other examples of non-tactile textures. Look in magazines, art books etc.

Observe and Discuss

When you have collected samples of non-tactile texture, study them carefully. Discuss the ways in which the non-tactile appearances were created.

Signpost

See *The Arnolfini Wedding*, page 118.

The Kitchen Maid, Jan Vermeer (1632–1675). Rijksmuseum, Amsterdam.

Great piece of turf: Study of weeds, Albrecht Dürer (1471–1528). Watercolour. Albertina Graphic Collection, Vienna.

Support Studies

These artists used raised blobs of paint to create a textured surface.

Study after Deposition by Rembrandt II, Frank Auerbach (1931 –). Private collection.

The Starry Night, Vincent van Gogh (1853–1890). Oil on canvas. 73 x 92cm (29 x 36¹/₄ in.). The Museum of Modern Art, New York. Lillie P. Bliss Bequest.

Frieze, Jackson Pollock (1912–1956). Christie's Colour Library, London.

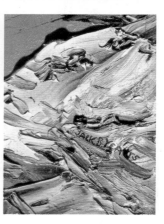

About to write a letter, Jack B. Yeats (1871–1957). Oil on canvas. National Gallery of Ireland. The two details of this painting show how Yeats used thick raised blobs of oil paint to create texture.

Printed textures — Students' work

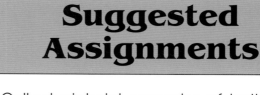

Texture created with sponge and paint (above) and with string and chipboard (right).

Suggested Assignments

1. Collect pictorial examples of both natural and manmade textures — for example, running water, snow, birds, grasses, clouds, slates, stone walls, trees, leaves etc.
2. Collect examples of wallpaper and fabric showing different forms of texture.
3. Make a 'feely board' by combining examples of both natural and manmade textures. Include steel wool, feathers, sandpaper, nuts and so forth.
4. Produce a chart showing various forms of drawn and brush textures. Use such materials as pencil, pen, crayon, paint etc.

Form and Space

A **form** is a shape that either *looks* 3-dimensional (3D) or which *is* 3D. Form is usually associated with sculpture and architecture, although it may also describe natural landscape features.

Natural forms.

Organic form, Clodagh Holahan. Clay sculpture.

Feminism, Clodagh Holahan. Sculpture in bronze on limestone.

The Eiffel Tower, Paris.

Bryce Canyon, Arizona, USA.

Observe and Discuss

Look at these examples of form — both natural and manmade. Talk about what you see.

We expect form to be *regular* or *balanced* in some way. It is easier to understand form when we think of something which is *formless* — it is something that is *shapeless*, like fire or clouds.

Space

Space describes the distance between people and places or objects.

Circle of Time, a sculpture by Joan Walsh-Smith and Charles Smith, shows how modern sculpture can dominate space.

Signposts

For more about the illusion of space, see Perspective, page 134.
See *Autumn Cannibalism,* page 12.
See *Circle of Time,* page 280.

Drawing

Self-portrait, Leonardo da Vinci (1452–1519).
Biblioteca Reale, Turin, Italy.

Support Studies

Drawing through the Ages

Since the beginning of time, people have felt the urge to draw — to make some kind of mark. The very first drawing was probably done in the sand with a pointed stick. Of course, such a drawing was not permanent. But once people learned to make dyes or inks from plants or minerals, they could leave marks in the world which would last. Some early human drawings have survived for thousands of years.

Signpost

See Painting, page 142.

As long ago as 10,000 BC, prehistoric people drew this picture deep inside a cave at Lascaux, France. It shows a sorcerer killing a buffalo.

Observe and Discuss

Study these drawings and talk about them. Can you see any differences in style through the years?

The Minoan civilisation flourished on the island of Crete around 1500 BC. The palace at Knossos was decorated with many frescoes, such as this one showing two blue dolphins.

Before Columbus arrived in the New World, the Mixtec people lived in what is now Mexico. This drawing from the 12th century AD shows warriors with animal masks.

Anyone can draw!

Anyone can learn to draw. Like driving or playing the piano, it is a skill which can be learned. It involves looking, common sense — and a lot of practice. The skill of drawing touches on many aspects of art, craft and design. Like the great genius Leonardo da Vinci, drawing can become a way of thinking, investigating or expressing yourself. Your hand — together with your eyes — will become an extension of your brain and heart. Marvellous things will begin to happen when you have learned to co-ordinate these things.

Untrained students' attempts at drawing chairs.

This chair was drawn by a student who had more practice. It is much more full of life.

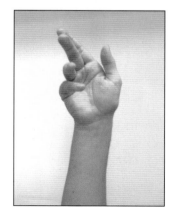

As your skills increase, your ability to draw what you see will also increase. Try not to rely too much on memory in the beginning. It can be a poor substitute for drawing an actual object, person or place. In time, you will develop your own way of drawing. But first, we must learn to see.

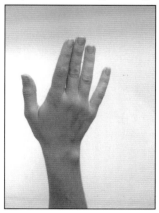

I know I have five fingers — but I don't always see all five of them in the same way. **Draw what you *see*, not what you know to be there**.

What is drawing?

A drawing is an image in which the main element is line. Drawing is the most immediate way of showing an object, an idea or a feeling in a pictorial way. This is done by using any tool or material that makes a mark. Drawing is basic to all forms of visual art, craft and design.

Preliminary study for *Terranova Madonna*, Raphael Sanzio (1483–1520).

A working drawing of a woman's head by Michelangelo (1475–1564). British Museum, London.

A working drawing in pencil by Clodagh Holahan.

Some drawings are called **working drawings** or **sketches**. They are the ideas, plans and preparations for paintings, packaging, design work and craft work.

The finished drawing in watercolour and gouache by Clodagh Holahan.

Drawing materials

You can draw with many things — pencils, charcoal, pens, inks, crayons, pastels, chalks, felt-tip markers, brushes, a stick, even a piece of cardboard dipped into paint or ink. The drawing material you use will depend on you, and the effect you want to create.

Imagine drawing with tape! That's what *Sony* did in their advertisement featuring Marilyn Monroe.

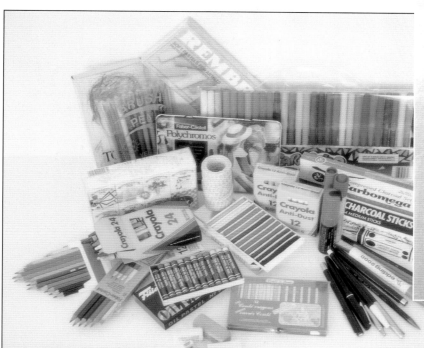

Students can choose from a wide variety of drawing materials.

A string drawing on a black background.

Suggested Assignment

Why not try drawing with all of these materials to see which ones you like best?

Pencils

Pencils are very popular for drawing. They vary in their **hardness** or **softness** and the kinds of marks they make.

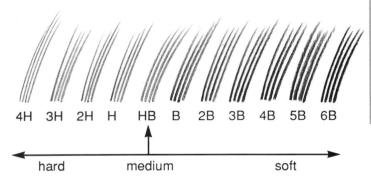

4H 3H 2H H HB B 2B 3B 4B 5B 6B

hard   medium   soft

Students used a variety of pencil grades to make these drawings of shells.

Hard pencils give a light and exact mark. They are suitable for precise work such as architectural or technical drawing.

Soft pencils give a dark, smooth mark. They are ideal for drawing.

Using a pencil also means that you can rub out or erase any marks you don't like. This means that you can achieve an in-depth and exact drawing. Remember, however, that always relying on the eraser can have its disadvantages. If you rely on it too much, it can lead to time-wasting or the loss of spontaneity.

Paper quality also plays an important part in drawing. The hardness or softness of the pencil mark will vary according to the surface on which it is used.

Remember the string portrait on page 97? This is a pencil portrait of the same person.

Suggested Assignment

Observe and Discuss

Try drawing with as many pencil grades as you can.

What did you discover through experimenting with different pencils?

Paper

There are many types of paper available, from very thin newsprint to heavy card. Try out as many types as you can. Try smooth as well as textured surfaces.

Your sketch pad

For your personal sketch pad, choose a reasonable-quality cartridge paper. The size should be either A4 or A3.

To begin with
- weight — 90 – 130 grams
- pencils — HB/2B – 3B/4B

Don't forget — you can draw on any type of paper — and on all sorts of surfaces. You can use any tool that will make a mark. Try as many combinations as you can!

A selection of paper, showing different weights, sizes and colours.

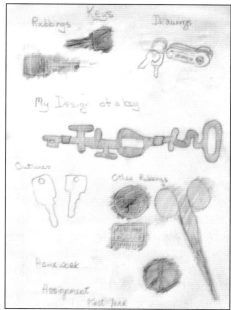

A sample of a page in a student's sketch pad.

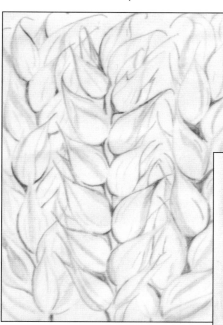

More work from students' sketch pads.

Other drawing materials

Once you have got used to using a pencil, try to be a bit more adventurous!

A **ball point pen** or a **marker** would present some challenges. You must think and look carefully before you make a mark. With these drawing tools, there is no going back!

Crayon gives a good, rough-textured look to a drawing.

Pastels can be blended and smudged to blur the lines. They are usually chalk- or oil-based.

Two portraits drawn with ball point pen.

A charcoal still life.

A crayon portrait.

Charcoal

Charcoal is a special type of burnt wood which is commonly used for drawing. It gives a definite or textured black line. Charcoal comes in assorted sizes. When smudged, it can give a shaded effect. This is called **sfumato**.

Before starting a specific drawing or project, it is always a good idea to experiment with any new material. This will help you to discover its strengths and weaknesses.

A pastel drawing.

Ink

Any sort of pen can be used for drawing. But don't forget that you can use a brush with ink. This can create a wonderful free effect. Many types of pens, brushes and inks are available.

For very precise work, you might choose a fine-tipped pen. These come in a wide variety of sizes. Most stationery and art shops will let you try out their range of pens before deciding what to buy.

A pen-and-ink drawing.

Felt-tipped pens

These pens come in a wide variety of sizes, colours and types.

Two studies created with felt-tipped pens.

Approaches to drawing

There are many types of drawing. There are also so many approaches to drawing that it is impossible to say whether one approach is better than another. There are so many things which affect the outcome of a drawing that there can be no hard and fast rules.

What should you consider when drawing?

Both the drawing materials used and the surfaces on which they are put will affect the finished drawing. So will the subject matter — whether it is natural or manmade, for example. The texture and the light and colour must all be considered.

Techniques

When a tonal effect is desired (to give a more three-dimensional quality), any of these techniques may be used.

- **Blending or smudging**
  with a cloth or finger

- **Cross hatching**
  making tiny criss-cross lines

- **Scribble hatching**
  building up with scribble lines

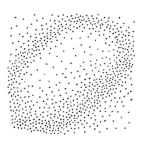

- **Pointillism**
  tiny dots clustered together in shady areas

- **Planes**
  blocks of different tone

Suggested Assignments

Try a drawing using each of these techniques, on different surfaces, to see which suits you best.

What should you draw?

Draw a subject — a person, thing, place or animal — that means something to you. You may wish to incorporate your chosen theme.

Where to start

Begin by drawing an object — either natural or manmade — which is not moving. This **still life** may be a vase of flowers or a basket of fruit, a skull, shells, a telephone, a group of bottles — the list is endless!

So many objects can be chosen as the subject of a still life.

A variety of still life drawings done by students.

More still life drawings by students

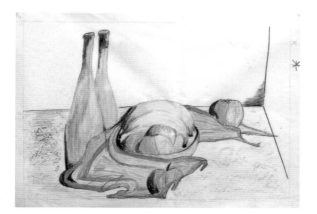

Bottles, vases, fruit and flowers — perfect for a still life.

Is a cat a good subject for a still life?

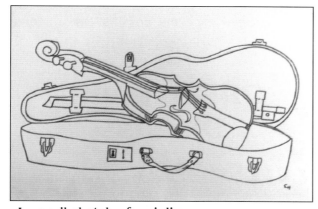

A pencil sketch of a violin.

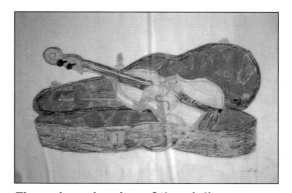

The colour drawing of the violin.

Students' still life ideas —13-15 years

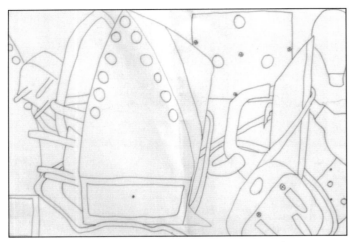

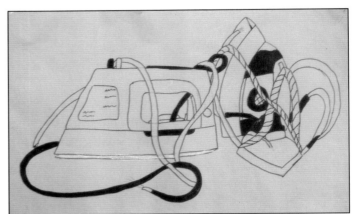

Household appliances can be interpreted in many ways.

This student saw excellent possibilities in a sheep's skull.

Observe and Discuss

1. What are the advantages of beginning with still life? Are there any disadvantages?
2. Look at a variety of still life paintings and drawings.

Observe and Discuss

Look carefully at how these artists have approached their wildlife subjects.

Butterflies, Phillip Gosse.
Watercolour.

Hare, Albrecht Dürer (1471–1528). Watercolour.
Albertina Graphic Collection, Vienna.

Elephant drawing, Rembrandt (1606–1669). Albertina Graphic Collection, Vienna.

Format

Place the object directly in front of you. In this way, you will know you are looking at your subject from the same angle each time you look at it.

Now decide whether your subject would look better **vertically** (called **portrait**) or **horizontally** (**landscape**). This will tell you how to turn your sketchbook or sheet of paper. A **viewfinder** will help you make this decision.

Making a viewfinder

Cut a rectangular shape in a piece of black paper or heavy card. The black helps to blot out anything which is beside your subject and gives you a clear outline. This simple viewfinder may also help you to arrange or position your subject in a more interesting way. If you are on location and do not have a viewfinder, you can always improvise.

Signpost

See Composition, pages 154, 163.

Horizontal - Landscape.

Vertical - Portrait.

Use your hands as a viewfinder or . . .

. . . make a viewfinder from black card or paper

Many people start to draw at the top of the paper and work their way down. But there is no rule to stop you from beginning in the middle, at the side or at the bottom. Experiment to find out what suits you best.

106

Types of drawing

Contour drawings

Contour drawings are the most common form of finished drawings. The outlines and edges reduce the subject matter to a very few lines. Such drawings are full of confidence and clarity. They are nearly always accurate interpretations of the subject.

Depending on the artist, contour drawings can be done very quickly, with one line and without much detail. Sometimes such drawings are called **pure line drawings**.

Signpost

See Picasso, page 109.

Still life, Henri Matisse (1869–1954).

Students' contour drawings

A pure line drawing.

This colour contour drawing of an apple was done with pastels.

Gesture drawings

Gesture drawings usually show a movement or an action which is taking place. They are usually done on 'the spur of the moment', capturing a fleeting scene. These drawings are often called **sketches** — rough plans which include some form of movement. They are rarely meant to be finished drawings. They are sometimes used as preparatory drawings before doing a painting.

Contour and gesture drawings are often intertwined. This gives a mixture of both techniques. It makes the drawing lively and spontaneous.

A student's gesture drawing on the theme 'The Wind'.

La danse, Henri Matisse (1869–1954). Musée de Grenoble. Photographiè: Musée de Grenoble/André Morin.

Observe and Discuss

What impresses you about this drawing by Pablo Picasso?

A line drawing by Pablo Picasso.

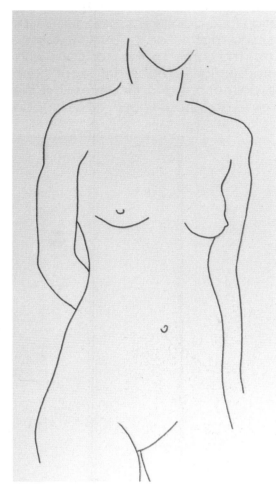

Line drawing, Clodagh Holahan.

Linear drawings

This type of drawing is called a **linear drawing** as it is made up entirely of lines. It is also a **finished drawing**. It was not drawn as a preparation for a painting, craft design or piece of sculpture. The drawing is an end in itself.

Suggested Assignment

Look at finished drawings by other artists. You will find many in magazines and newspapers.

Drawings by other artists

A **cartoon** is a full-size drawing made in preparation for a painting or some other work of art such as a mosaic or tapestry. These cartoons are not the same as the cartoons with which we are familiar — modern cartoons are comic strips, animations or caricatures. This sketch by Leonardo da Vinci is known as a cartoon.

Cartoon for *Virgin and Child with St Anne*, Leonardo da Vinci (1452–1519). National Gallery, London.

Four dancers in a landscape, a pastel sketch by Edgar Degas (1834–1917). Private collection.

Reclining figure, study for a sculpture in wood by Henry Moore (1898–1986). Private collection.

Suggested Assignment

Your skills of observation will increase with practice. Why not try to take different views of the same objects? In trying this, you will be in good company. Leonardo da Vinci kept many notebooks and sketches. He used them as required in his paintings, rather than having to start from scratch each time he wanted to paint a picture.

Observe and Discuss

Look at the work of Leonardo da Vinci and discuss his approach to drawing.

Portraits

A **portrait** is the likeness of a real person. It may be drawn, painted or photographed. When beginning a portrait, don't be too concerned about getting an exact likeness straight away. Try to get the 'feel' of the shape of the face before you try exact details of that face.

Le Petit Dejeuner, Sarah Purser (1848–1943). National Gallery of Ireland.

Students' early attempts at portraiture

More advanced work

All you need to begin your attempts at portraiture is someone who will sit still for 10–15 minutes at a time. Then concentrate on getting the proportions of the head and shoulders right. Using a large sheet of drawing paper, try to get the head and shoulders about the same size as the actual person. Try different media — pencil, ballpoint pen, crayon. Try front and side views.

Don't worry if your first attempts at portraiture look a little strange. For example, many people tend to put the eyes too high on the face. This is quite understandable, as we tend to look people straight in the eyes. We don't take much notice of the forehead.

Proportions of the head

In order to place the features in their correct positions, try to analyse the head and work out the proportions within the face. This can be done by following a few simple rules.

The face and the head

One of the best ways of getting to know the structure of the face is to feel your own face. Notice the hard parts — the bones — and the soft parts — the hollows.

Front view

1. The head is egg-shaped.
2. The widest part of the head is above the temples.
3. The eyes are in the centre and 'hang' from the centre line. The distance between the eyes equals the width of one eye (an eye is $\frac{1}{5}$ of the distance across the face).
4. Half-way between the eyes and the chin is the end of the nose.
5. The ears occupy the same space at either side of the face.
6. The mouth is at least the width of the nose and is nearer the nose than the chin.

Side view

1. The side face resembles an egg, with a small section added on.
2. The upper lip cuts through the nostrils. It also projects out farther than the lower lip.
3. The eye slopes backwards.
4. The ear begins from the jawline and occupies the same length as the nose.
5. The end of the nose, the end of the ear and the nape of the neck are in line.
6. The jaw is a square curve.

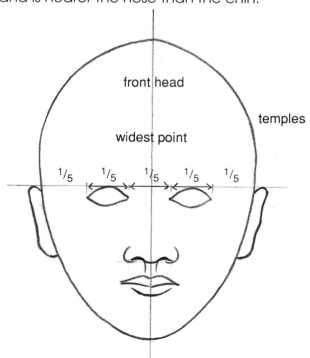

front head

temples

widest point

$\frac{1}{5}$ $\frac{1}{5}$ $\frac{1}{5}$ $\frac{1}{5}$ $\frac{1}{5}$

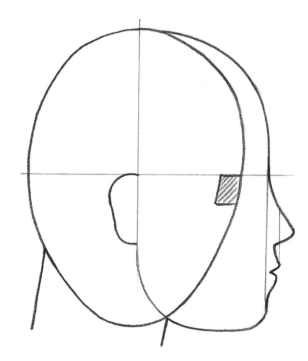

Feature details

When you have mastered the proportions of the face, try to take each feature and practise it separately. Remember that no one has exactly the same features as someone else, but the basic structure is the same.

(close up)
Remember that the eye is about the size of a golf ball.

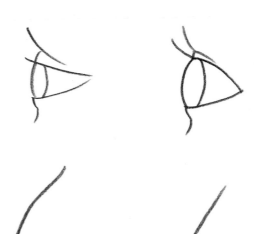

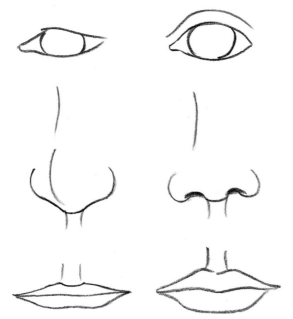

Front View

Side View

Profile - structure.

Profile - tones.

Self-portraits

It's always fun to do your own self-portrait. Just get a large mirror and set yourself up.

A student and her self-portrait.

A later self-portrait.

This student's self-portrait was achieved by using a mirror and a pencil.

Suggested Assignments

Experimenting with the light source

Place a lamp beside your model. (It could be a self-portrait, if you have a large mirror.) Move the light slightly behind the model. Then move it slightly to the front. Note what happens to the shadows on the face when you move the light source.

For a more eerie lighting effect, hold a torch directly below the face and then directly above the face. The shadows will give a distorted view of the face. Draw these views of the face and then keep them in your sketchbook. You may find them useful if you are doing a project on video covers for something like horror movies!

Signpost

See special effects, page 3.

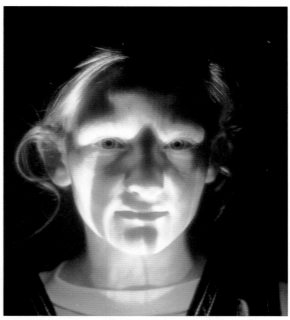

Create creepy shadows by holding a torch under your chin!

Note how the shadows on the face are exaggerated in this self-portrait.

The Penitent Magdalene, Georges de La Tour (1593–1652). The Louvre, Paris.
Comment on the effect of the light source in this painting.

A famous portrait

The Arnolfini Wedding Portrait, 1434. Oil on panel. National Gallery, London.

Jan van Eyck (1390–1441)

This famous portrait was painted to celebrate the marriage between Giovanni Arnolfini and Giovanna Cerami. Here are a few things to note about this portrait.

* Arnolfini is about to place his right hand into hers — a sign of their marriage.

* The single candle in the chandelier is a sign of God's presence.
* The bride is wearing green — the symbol of affection.
* Her little dog is a sign of her faithfulness.
* The mirror shows the reflection of the witnesses — so the ceremony is a legal contract.
* Above the mirror, van Eyck has written, in Latin, 'Jan van Eyck was here', making the picture a legal document.
* The shoes represent hallowed ground.
* Around the mirror are ten scenes from the Passion of Christ, showing how important religion is to the couple.
* The marriage bed is in the background.

Famous Self-portraits

Rembrandt (1606–1669). Probably one of the greatest painters of self-portraits. He painted his own image at least ninety times.

Francis Bacon (1909–1992). This artist does not like verbal explanations of his work. He wants his paintings to speak for themselves.

Vincent van Gogh (1853–1890). This portrait shows his bandaged head after he had cut off his ear. Vincent actually cut off his left ear—he painted this picture looking in a mirror.

Different artists' approaches to portraits

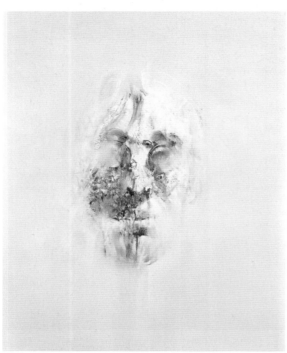

Louis le Brocquy (1916 -) *Study towards an image of W. B. Yeats* (1976).

Kuniyoshi
Girl scolding a thieving cat (1845). Woodblock print.

Baldassare Peruzzi (1481–1536). *Portrait of Ceres.*

Edward McGuire (1932–1986). *Portrait of Seamus Heaney.*

Observe and Discuss

1. Look again at the portraits done by famous artists in this section. Then choose: (a) the one you like best; (b) the one you like least; (c) the one you find the most interesting. Give at least three reasons to support your opinions.
2. Which of these artists would you have chosen to paint your portrait? Why would you choose this artist?

120

Vincent van Gogh (1853–1890).
L'arlesienne.

Giuseppe Archimboldo (1527–1593).
Water, 1566. This artist also did portraits entitled *Summer* and *Winter*. He used fruit, vegetables and other everyday objects in his 'portraits'.

Brian Bourke (1936–   ).
Self-portrait and Don Quixote (1980).

Robert Ballagh (1943–   ).
Homage to Bernadette Greevy (1978). The singer is surrounded by symbols of her work and interests.

Silhouettes: A type of portraiture

Before the advent of photography, portraits (either paintings or drawings) were the only way of recording a person's image. **Silhouettes** are another way of presenting the human form.

A silhouette of the composer, Ludwig van Beethoven made in 1903 by Selipmann. Beethoven House, Vienna.

A silhouette is a dark shape showing a definite outline against a lighter background. This is called a **positive image**. With every positive image there is a corresponding **negative image** — in this case, the background.

They became very popular during Victorian times when silhouettes were cut from black paper to show the sitter's profile.

Signposts

See Pattern, page 44.
See Stencil printing, page 186.
See Photography, page 242.

Silhouettes can be ambiguous! Is it two faces — or a vase?

Suggested Assignment

To create your own silhouette portrait, project the shadow of your sitter onto a sheet of paper. Outline the shadow carefully. Then cut it out.

Negatives and Positives

1. Get a sheet of white paper and a sheet of black paper which is half the size of the white.

2. Place the black sheet over the white one. You immediately have a positive and a negative.

3. Now cut the black sheet in two with a crooked line.

4. Flick over and stick down the black pieces onto the white paper.

From portraits to face painting

Using our knowledge of portraiture, we will now look at face painting. To be successful, face painting must take account of the proportions of the face.

We often associate face painting with primitive tribes. But it is also very popular now with young people at fairgrounds and parties.

The face painting of this Surma warrior follows the contours of his face.

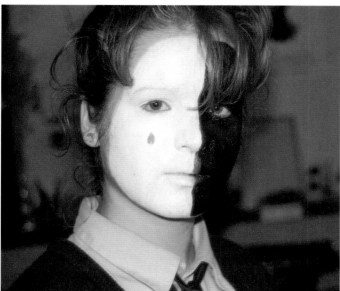

Signpost

See Surma warrior, page 44.

123

Masks

Chinese dragon masks are worn during the Chinese New Year celebrations.

Tutankhamun's gold death mask is thought to be an exact likeness of this pharaoh.

Elaborate masks are associated with Venice, as they are often worn there during the famous Carnival of Venice which takes place before Lent each year.

This wooden face mask from Zaire represents a female spirit or ghost.

This wooden mask is worn by members of a secret society in Nigeria. It shows the face of a leper below a human skull.

A colourful collection of masks from around the world.

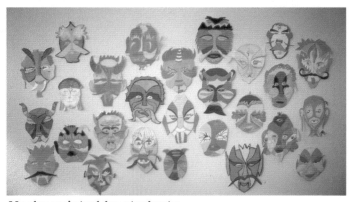

Masks painted by students.

Caricatures

Caricatures are distorted portraits which usually exaggerate certain characteristics in a person. For example, if a person has a big nose or bushy eyebrows, these might be highlighted by the caricaturist. The main targets of the caricature are politicians, film stars, pop singers — almost anyone in public life.

Caricatures are found mainly in newspapers and certain magazines. They tend to be unflattering, but can also be extremely funny. The subject of the caricature must always be recognisable.

The TV programme 'Spitting Image' is famous for its puppet caricatures. In using these three-dimensional figures, they have taken the art of the caricature one step further. They have also shown that all puppetry is not simply of the 'Punch and Judy' type.

Suggested Assignment

Look in magazines and newspapers for examples of caricature. Make a display of your examples.

Observe and Discuss

Can you see particular styles in the work of each caricature artist? Can you recognise a particular artist by his/her style?

Signpost

See *Autumn Cannibalism,* page 12.

George Bernard Shaw, the Irish writer, a caricature by Sir Bernard Partridge. Comment on the impression of Shaw given in this image.

The actor Sean Connery by Michael ffolkes. Discuss whether any features are exaggerated.

The Surrealist painter, Salvador Dali, by Richard Cole. This caricature uses images from Dali's own work.

The Human Figure

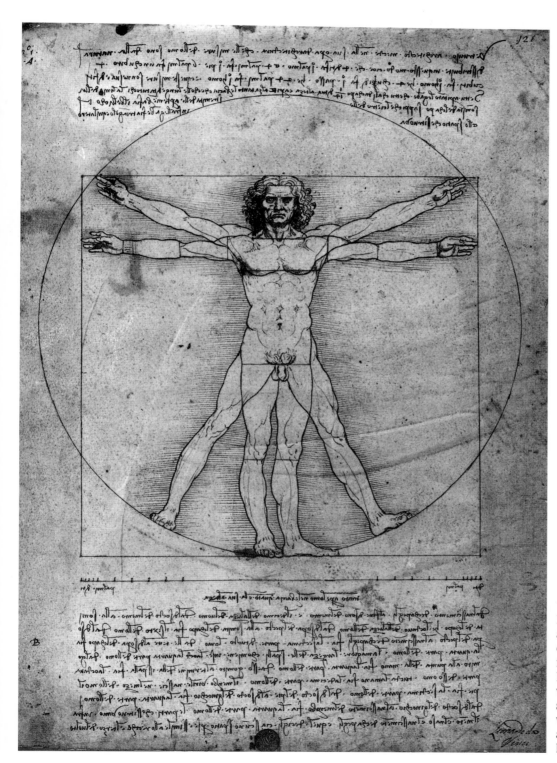

The Golden Section, by Leonardo da Vinci, shows a carefully worked out drawing of the human figure in exact proportion. Leonardo's notes are written in his own curious style of 'mirror writing', which makes it difficult for anyone else to interpret his thoughts.

Figure drawing

Observe and Discuss

As a first attempt at figure drawing, draw a figure of a person standing from memory. Try to analyse your drawing. What are its good points? Are there features of this that are not as successful as you would like them to be?

Now get someone else to pose for you — again standing up. Analyse this drawing. How is it different from the one you drew from memory?

Students' early attempts at figure drawings.

Suggested Assignment

Now get together with a few of your friends and work out the proportions of the human figure. Get several large pieces of paper — sheets of newspaper will do — and stick them together. Get one of your friends to lie down and trace around him/her on the paper (see photos below).

When you have finished drawing around the person's body, fold the paper in half width-wise. This will show you exactly where the middle of the body is. Then measure the length of the head (from forehead to chin). See how many times the length of the head 'goes into' the length of the entire body. (Divide the head length into the body length.)

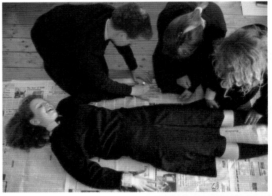

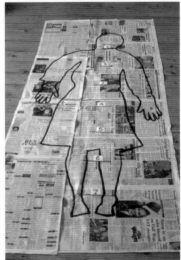

128

You should have discovered a few things.
- The half-way line is on the hips.
- The head goes into the body about 7.5 times (this may vary slightly with each person).

Here are a few other guidelines you can use.
Remember!
1. The distance across the head = the distance from the neck to the shoulders.
2. The elbows come to the waist.
3. When spread, a hand covers the face.
4. The finger tips reach the middle of the thigh.
5. Limbs get smaller as they go away from the body.
6. The feet are larger than the hands.

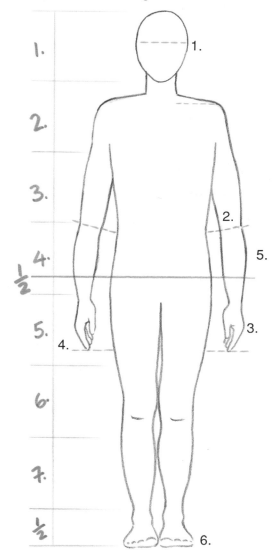

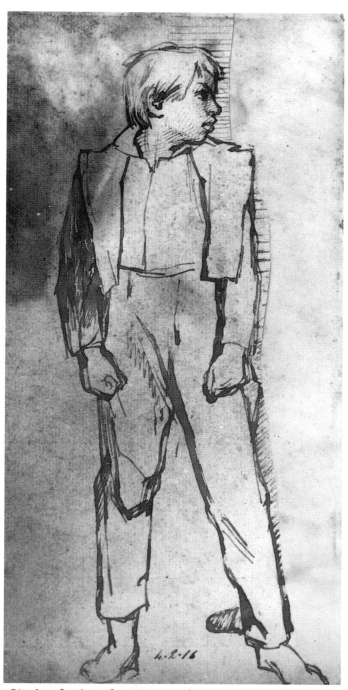

Study of a boy for 'The Wolf and the Lamb', William Mulready (1786–1863). Pen and brown ink. The Whitworth Art Gallery, Manchester.

Foreshortening

Foreshortening is a technique which gives the impression of depth. The illustrations below and on page 131 will help you to understand this concept.

Side view of seated girl. Note the side of the upper leg.

Front view of a seated girl. Notice how her upper legs are hidden from view. This is a good example of foreshortening.

Signpost

Look at 'The Pointing Posters', pages 220-21. Discuss how they show foreshortening.

Suggested Assignment

Put someone in a foreshortened pose. Now draw this pose.

Front view of a standing girl.

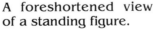

A foreshortened view of a standing figure.

A student's drawing showing a foreshortened pose.

To be aware of foreshortening, you must be very observant. You must learn to draw what you actually see, not what you know is there.

Support Studies

Supper at Emmaus was painted around 1598 by the Italian artist, Caravaggio (1573–1610). It provides us with a number of examples of foreshortening. On the left, the elbow of the man in green is clearly foreshortened. So are the hands and arms of Christ and of the apostle on the right.

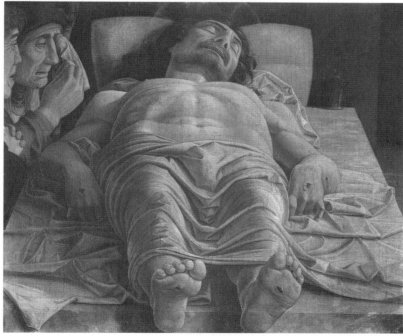

The Dead Christ was painted around 1465 by Andrea Mantegna (1431–1506). It exhibits his lack of knowledge of foreshortening. For example, Christ's feet are about the same size as the hand of the weeping woman (top left). What else do you notice?

Suggested Assignment

Instead of excluding hands and feet from your drawings, practise them separately until you have mastered their forms.

Use your own hand to make gestures such as making a fist and pointing. Draw these poses.
Try drawing some functional poses.
- holding a pen or pencil
- holding a teapot or cup
- holding a scissors
- holding a spoon or fork
- holding a bottle or tin

Now draw your foot.
- Draw your bare foot.
- Now draw your foot with the sock on.
- Draw your foot with your shoe on.

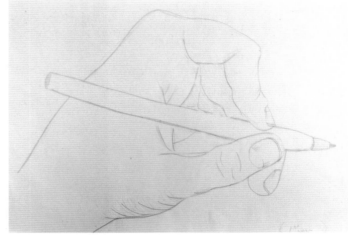

A student's drawing of a functional pose.

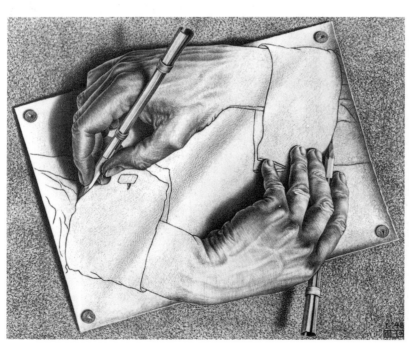

Drawing Hands, M.C. Escher (1898–1972). Lithograph.©1948. M.C. Escher Foundation, Baarn, Holland.

Hands, Albrecht Dürer (1471–1528). Albertina, Vienna.

Action poses

When you have practised drawing the still figure, why not try some action poses?

The best way to do this is to observe someone while they are performing some activity — walking, running, digging, sweeping, cleaning windows, ironing. Then get someone to 'freeze' in their actions so you can draw them.

It can be fun and challenging to get three or four people to walk about in a group in front of you. Their bodies will be overlapping and intertwining. Try to draw the action only. You won't be able to get details — just a feeling of movement. Be sure the limbs bend in a normal way — elbows bend upwards and forwards; legs bend forward from the hip and backward from the knee.

Support Studies

The painting by Marcel Duchamp is called *Nude Descending a Staircase* (1919). Note the action of the figure as she walks down the stairs.

Balla's painting of a dog gives a wonderful impression of action.

Nude Decending a Staircase No. 2, Marcel Duchamp (1881–1955). Philadelphia Museum of Art, Louise and Walter Arenberg Collection.

Dynamism of a Dog on a Leash, Giacomo Balla (1871–1958). Oil on canvas. Albright Knox Art Gallery, Buffalo, New York.

A student's action drawing.

Perspective

Perspective is a way of showing distance in a drawing or painting.

To make the subject of a drawing or painting appear in the correct proportions, we must use perspective. Perspective is all about creating an illusion — a 3-dimensional appearance on a 2-dimensional surface. We want to create the illusion that things get smaller as they go farther away from us. Of course, objects don't really get smaller — they just seem to. In our drawings and paintings, we must learn to use perspective if the drawing is going to look real. We must also consider colour when using perspective. Colours change with distance. They appear to grow paler, creating an impression of depth and distance.

We know that the railway tracks do not meet, although they may seem to as they go into the distance. Perspective shows how objects in the distance (e.g. the sleepers under the tracks) *appear* to be smaller than ones that are nearer.

Suggested Assignment

Imagine you are standing in the middle of the road. There are houses on one side and trees on the other. Now draw this scene.

Observe and Discuss

The drawings above were made by 12–13 year old students with no prior knowledge of perspective.

134

One-point perspective

If you draw a railway track or straight road — like the one in the picture at the right — you will notice that the sides of the road seem to meet in the distance, even though we know they are parallel lines. The place at which the lines seem to meet is called the **vanishing point**. Vanishing points are often on the horizon. You can also have vanishing points above and below the horizon line. The position of the horizon in your picture depends on your eye level.

Note how the trees in the distance seem to be smaller.

All of these illustrations show different eye levels.
View 1: A bird's eye view — viewed from the air.
View 2: The normal view — viewed from human eye level, standing.
View 3: A worm's eye view — viewed from the ground.

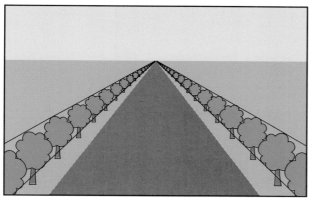

View 1: A bird's eye view - viewed from the air.

View 2: The normal view - viewed from human eye level, standing.

View 3: A worm's eye view - viewed from the ground.

135

Two-point perspective

Everything we look at has perspective, not just roads and railway lines. Perspective, however, is not always this obvious. Some pictures and scenes may have more than one vanishing point. This is called **two-point perspective**.

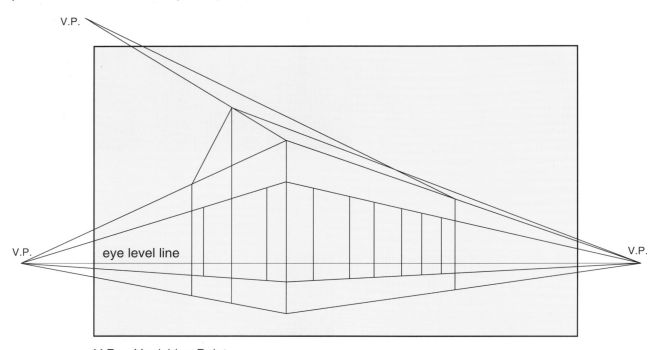

V.P. = Vanishing Point

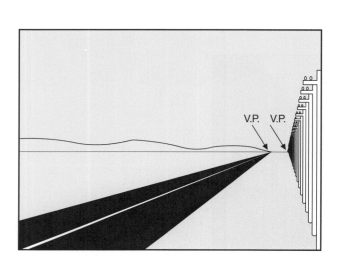

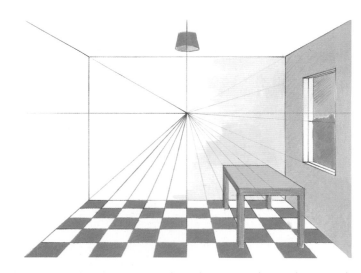

All lines above the eye level come down to meet at the vanishing point. All lines below come up to meet the eye level line at the vanishing point.

136

Perspective and ellipses

Whatever you are drawing, the main thing to remember is to draw your subject from the same position, angle or viewpoint.

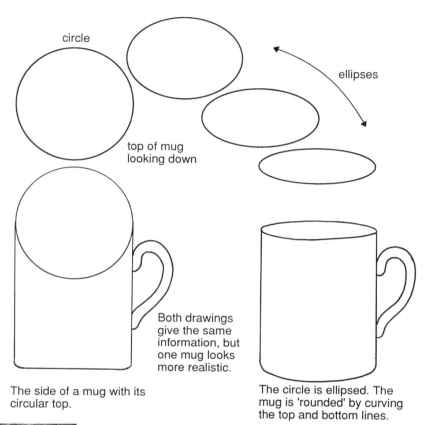

circle

ellipses

top of mug
looking down

Both drawings give the same information, but one mug looks more realistic.

The side of a mug with its circular top.

The circle is ellipsed. The mug is 'rounded' by curving the top and bottom lines.

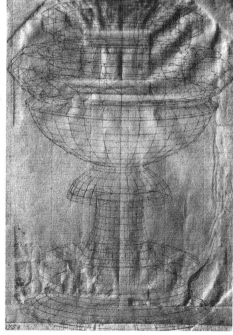

Perspective drawing of a chalice, Paolo Uccello (1397–1475). It seems that Uccello was obsessed with the study of perspective. Even his close friend, the sculptor Donatello, laughed at him. Because of work by people like Uccello, however, artists who studied his work were able to achieve greater realism in their work.

Support Studies

Perspective seems so obvious to us. Once we know about it, it seems so logical. But this was not always the case. During the Byzantine Period (10th – 13th centuries), paintings lacked perspective. Pictures tended to be stiff, flat, formal and symbolic, as the *Virgin and Child* painting shows. They had no depth, and figures seemed to float against the flat backgrounds.

Giotto (1266–1337) was a Florentine painter and architect. He was the first artist to use perspective, although the rules of perspective were not worked out until nearly a hundred years later.

Signposts

See Dali, page 152.
See Piero della Francesca, page 159.
See Giotto, page 159.

The Virgin and Child, with John the Baptist and Twelve Prophets, Constantinople School, 1325. Tempera on panel. National Gallery of Ireland.

The Vision of Joachim, Giotto (1266–1337). Fresco. Arena Chapel, Padua.

138

Examples of Perspective

The Avenue, Middelharnis, Meyndert Hobbema (1638–1709). National Gallery, London.

A student's drawing after learning about perspective.

The artist's bedroom at Arles, Vincent van Gogh (1853–1890). Musée d'Orsay, Paris.

139

Observe and Discuss

. . . the print by Hogarth. At the bottom of the print, the artist has written:

Whoever makes a design, without the knowledge of perspective, will be liable to such absurdities as are shown in this print. Comment on these absurdities.

Artists such as M.C. Escher distorted perspective. To do this successfully, however, you must know what you are distorting and why, and how to go about it.

W. Hogarth, Pinx.   *J. Moore, Sculp.*

WHOEVER MAKES A DESIGN, WITHOUT THE KNOWLEDGE OF PERSPECTIVE,
WILL BE LIABLE TO SUCH ABSURDITIES AS ARE SHOWN IN THIS PRINT.

Perspective Study, William Hogarth (1697–1764). Engraving.

Relativity, M.C.Escher (1898–1972). Lithograph. ©1953 M.C. Escher Foundation, Baarn, Holland.

Painting

The Red House at Mougins, Grace Henry (1868–1953). Oil on canvas. National Gallery of Ireland.

What is painting?

Painting is the application of some type of colouring matter onto a flat surface.

In one way, painting can be seen as an extension of drawing, since both are about making marks on a flat surface. There are a few differences, however. Drawing is concerned with the linear quality of the 'mark'; painting sees the 'mark' in terms of tones, colours, shapes and textures as well as line. Also, drawings do not have to be an end in themselves, while paintings almost always are.

Why do people paint?

There are many answers to this question — as many answers as there are painters! In ancient times, painting was an important part of religious beliefs and practices. It also had a decorative role.

Cave dwellers often painted their prey before the hunt. Egyptians used art as part of their burial rites. Australian aborigines decorated caves and walls with paintings.

Signposts

See Drawing, page 94.
See *The Arnolfini Wedding*, page 118.
See *The Jewish Bride*, page 9.
See *The Battle of San Romano*, page 9.

Before the camera, artists used paintings as a means of recording some important event or person. They painted beautiful scenes, a street, possessions like horses, houses and land. They painted still lives, the interiors of houses and, of course, many things associated with religion.

Other artists painted as a means of expressing themselves. They wanted to communicate in some way, giving their own visual interpretations of themes such as heaven, hell, love or war. The most vivid and imaginative work was created by Hieronymus Bosch, as this painting shows.

The Garden of Earthly Delights (centre panel), Hieronymus Bosch (c.1450–1516). Oil on panel. Prado, Madrid.

Mares and Foals in a Landscape, George Stubbs (1724–1806). Tate Gallery, London.

Mr and Mrs Andrews, Thomas Gainsborough (1727–1788). National Gallery, London.

Modern artists paint pictures for many of the same reasons. Modern painting is probably more personal than it ever was.

The camera took away the need to make accurate records of things or people through paintings. It freed painters to respond more personally to their surroundings and their own inner thoughts. Artists paint what they feel. They experiment with different media through their art and try to find out more about colour, pattern, shape, line, texture and form. Sometimes modern artists deal with a particular subject. At other times they explore the materials they are using for their own sake.

The **Impressionists** were the first painters to break away from the more formal style of painting. Manet's painting of a train station, for example, is not a realistic image, but an impression of what he saw. During his time in Tahiti, Paul Gauguin painted portraits of Tahitian people which were very free and vibrant. Seurat also created his own impressions by using tiny dots of pure pigment—a style known as **pointillism.**

La Gare St Lazare, Claude Monet (1840–1926). Paris.

Et l'or de leur corps, Paul Gauguin (1848–1903). Musée du Louvre, Paris.

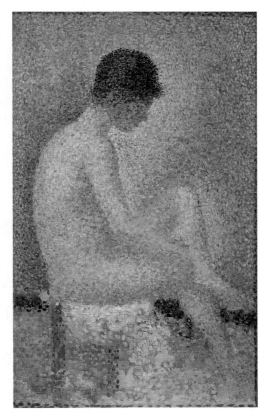

Profile of a model, George Seurat (1859–1891). Palais de Tokyo, Paris.

Signposts

See Impressionism, page 11.
See Pointillism, page 101.

Realism

Many artists paint exactly what is in front of them. This is called **realism**. Some artists are so accurate in their painting that their style is called **photo-realism**. Other artists, both past and present, compose pictures from their vivid imaginations. And other painters begin by looking at a person or thing and then re-arranging what they see. This is what **Cubist** painters did.

Cubism

Pablo Picasso (1881–1973), Juan Gris (1887–1927) and Georges Braque (1882–1963) simplified and reduced forms to geometric shapes. They tended to show all aspects of their chosen subject on one flat surface.

In *The Weeping Woman*, Picasso shows both the side view and front view of the woman in one picture.

Painters use **style**, **composition** and a variety of **materials** to express their individual ideas and talents. This is what makes each work unique.

Signpost

See Georges Braque, page 164.
See Pablo Picasso, pages 78, 150-51, 164-65.

Apples and oranges, Paul Cezanne (1839–1906). Musée d'Orsay, Paris.

The Weeping Woman, Pablo Picasso (1881–1973). Penrose Collection.

Large Red Interior, Henri Matisse (1869–1954). National Museum of Modern Art, Paris.

144

Woman and Two Bantam Cocks (1985). Watercolour and acrylic. Pauline Bewick.

If paint is bought in bulk, it is usually a powder paint or a redimix paint. The powder paints must be mixed with water. Redimix is already mixed and ready for use. Both of these paints are fairly cheap. They are also easy to use, and give quite good results.

If you buy your own paints, the popular choices are:
1. poster jars
2. solid paint discs
3. paint boxes of good-quality, with replacement tablets

It is recommended that all students have a supply of the following for assignments.
- A supply of paints — at least red, yellow, blue, black, white
- 3 brushes — numbers 2, 6 (soft hair) 10, or similar, flat hog hair
- 1 sketch pad — A4 or A3

All or some of the following are also needed.
- 1 packet of crayons/pastels/colouring pencils/ markers
- 2 soft pencils (HB/2B and 3B/4B)
- 1 soft eraser
- 1 notebook or exercise book

Painting materials

Paints

There are many types of paints available. The most commonly used ones are water-based. Among the many different types of paints are these.
- powder paint
- redimix (poster) paints
- tablet form of paints (in a box or on a tray) in disc or rectangular form
- poster paints
- gouache paints
- watercolour paints
- acrylic paints
- oil paints

Students can choose from a wide range of painting materials.

145

Professional paints

Gouache paints

These are often called 'designer's paints'. They give a flat and even finish. They consist of pigment and glue mixed with water. They are a bit expensive for everyday use.

Signpost

See Stamps, pages 232-235.

Watercolour paints

Good quality water colour paints can be very expensive. Water colours give a transparent look to a picture, but they are quite difficult to use properly. They are not really suitable for beginners.

Trees in the snow, William John Leech (1881– 1968). Watercolour with charcoal. National Gallery of Ireland.

Acrylic paints

Acrylic paints are plastic-based paints which are thinned down with water. They dry very quickly. Care must be taken of brushes when using acrylics. The brushes can deteriorate and become unusable if acrylics are left to dry on them. Acrylics are expensive for students. If they are used, they should be confined to special projects.

Signpost

See Pauline Bewick, page 145.

Oil paints

Oil paints are oil-based paints which are usually mixed with linseed oil, white spirits or turpentine. Oil paints are not recommended for general use, since they are so expensive. They also take a long time to dry. They are excellent for marbling. Oil paints are still the most popular paints.

Bus Stop, Martin Gale. Oil on canvas.

Palettes

A plate or bun tray will make a good palette if no proper painting palette is available. Palettes with plenty of small wells for mixing colours are more economical with paints. Large-welled palettes are good for mixing large quantities of paint.

Brushes

Brushes vary in both size and price. There are round and flat ones, with different types of hair, at a variety of prices. A sable brush is best, but it is also expensive. It is not really necessary for the beginner. Hog and squirrel-haired brushes are the most popular with students — these are quite adequate. Broad brushes are used for covering large areas quickly. They are especially useful for putting on a wash.

Each student should have access to no less than three brushes of the types mentioned earlier.

Signpost

See washes, page 149.

Care of paints, brushes and palettes

Wash all palettes and brushes immediately after use. Never leave brushes standing in water — this loosens the bristles. Always 'point' the hairs of a brush before putting it away — otherwise it will lose its shape.

When brushes are being stored for any length of time (as during the summer), they should be washed with soap, 'pointed', and then left to dry.

Taking a line for a walk — there are endless possibilities!

Paper

You can paint on just about any paper, although thicker paper gives better results. Many students use cartridge paper. This usually ranges in weight from 90 grams to 150 grams.

There is a special watercolour paper with a high quality texture. It is very absorbent, but also expensive.

Take care not to use too much water when applying paint to paper. Otherwise the paper will get very bumpy.

Suggested Assignments

1. Experiment with painting first by using different brush strokes.

Signpost

See Painting techniques, page 155.

2. Try 'taking a line for a walk' and then filling in the shapes which you have created. This will help you to practise painting without having to come up with an actual picture. With such an exercise, you will start learning to control the paint and the brush. It will also help you to learn how to mix the paints to an even consistency and to paint as evenly as possible. (The whole purpose of painting is not necessarily to paint with a smooth, even consistency — though it is a great training.)
3. Experiment with colour mixing to get a specific colour shade or tint. When mixing colours, always remember to start with a light colour — for example, start with yellow, then add red to get orange.
4. Try stippling (painting in dots or separate touches) or letting the colours flow into one another. This will give texture and movement to a picture.

Signpost

See Colour, page 28.

Observe and Discuss

Discuss this painting by Gillian Ayres under these headings: colour, movement, texture, technique, composition, impact.

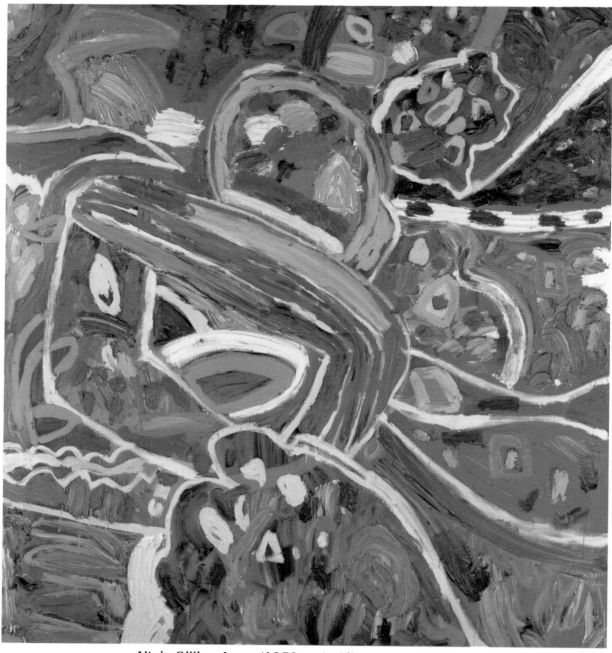

Altair, Gillian Ayres (1930 -   ). Oil on canvas. 244cm x 214cm (8ft x 7ft).
Purdy Hicks Gallery, London.

A wash

A wash is a watery mixture of paint. When a wash is applied to paper, it covers the surface fairly evenly. It can also be graded, giving a faintly textured background.

Method

1. Attach the paper to a board which is on a slant.
2. Start to apply paint at the top. Work your way from left to right across the sheet of paper with a loaded wet brush. With each brush stroke, make sure to catch the end of the previous stroke, working as evenly as possible.
3. You may also try using a sponge for this exercise.

Different background effects

Try different background effects using texture: (a) a sponge giving a stippled effect; (b) some crumpled paper dipped in paint; (c) a rag dipped in paint; (d) a roller coated with paint.

A wash.

Suggested Assignments

1. Do a plain wash.
2. Do a graded wash.

Marbling

For marbling, you will need:
    gelatine
    oil paints
    paint brush
    turpentine or white spirits
    a large, flat tray
    water
    paper (150 gram at least)

Method

1. Dissolve the gelatine in hot water (not boiling). Always add the gelatine to the water by adding a tablespoon of gelatine to each 1/2 litre of water. Enough should be prepared to fill the tray to 1/2 or 3/4.
2. Use as many colours of oil paint as you require. Mix each one separately with turpentine or white spirits until it is runny.
3. Drip the liquid oil paint or paints onto the surface of the water. (The paint should float.)
4. Stir or move the paint around on the water.
5. When you are happy with the appearance of the paint, place a sheet of paper on the surface of the water for a few seconds.
6. Slowly lift the paper from the liquid and leave to dry.

For added effect, you could use a special metal comb to break up the oil paint on the surface of the water. This will give different patterns.

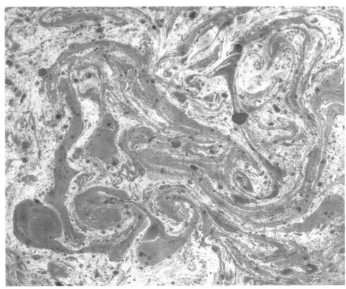

A marbling effect.

Painting a picture

First, do preparatory studies of your chosen theme.

When starting to paint a picture, it is a good idea to do research and make a plan first. This could be a miniature sketch of the proposed picture.

Plans should be drawn which take account of the format of your picture or paper — for example, landscapes are usually horizontal, while portraits are usually upright or vertical.

Signpost

See format, pages 71, 106.

Plans or sketches for a picture

You don't need to erase old plans — the miniature format allows plenty of space to sketch in new ideas. The plans should be kept safely for further reference. They are also useful for showing the development which took place to create the final image.

Signpost

See Preparatory Studies in the Table of Contents.

The meaning of *Guernica*
by Pablo Picasso

The Background

There was a civil war in Spain from 1936 to 1939. It was a very brutal and bloody war in which brother fought brother. The eventual winner of the war, Francisco Franco, ruled Spain as a dictator until his death in 1975.

In 1937, the aircraft of Condor Brigade, Franco's German allies, flew over the ancient town of Guernica and bombed it on market day. The bombing nearly destroyed the entire town. Many people were killed in the raging fires started by the bombing. Animals for sale in the market ran in terror as they too were being killed.

Pablo Picasso, a native of Spain, was by now living in France because he had spoken out against Franco. The bombing so enraged the great painter that he immediately began work on one of his most famous paintings — *Guernica*. In this enormous painting — 3.5m x 7.5m (11ft 5.5in. x 25ft 5.75in.), Picasso tried to show the horrors of war. The picture is full of animals and people, mainly women and children — the innocent victims, screaming in agony, horror and despair.

A portrait of Pablo Picasso taken in 1959 by Lee Miller.

Observe and Discuss

Look very carefully at Picasso's treatment of *Guernica* and talk about its impact. Do you feel that Picasso has succeeded in depicting the horrors of war?

Try to find other paintings of war and see how they compare with *Guernica*.

Guernica, Pablo Picasso (1881–1973). Oil on canvas. Queen Sofia Museum, Madrid. Picasso stated that *Guernica* should only return to Spain when Franco was dead. The dictator died in 1975 and the painting was returned to the Prado in Madrid in 1981. Late in 1992, Picasso's masterpiece was taken to the new Queen Sofia Museum.

The meaning of Guernica

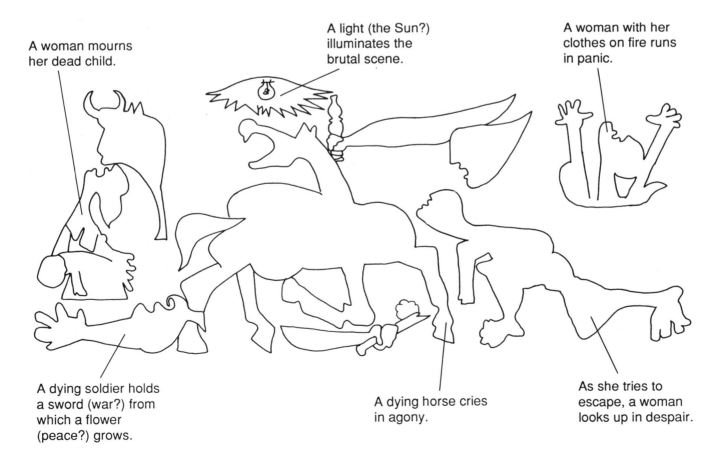

A woman mourns her dead child.

A light (the Sun?) illuminates the brutal scene.

A woman with her clothes on fire runs in panic.

A dying soldier holds a sword (war?) from which a flower (peace?) grows.

A dying horse cries in agony.

As she tries to escape, a woman looks up in despair.

Support Studies

Some modern art is often referred to as **abstract art**. This term is used to describe non-recognisable images which tend to rely mainly on the **art elements**.

Signpost

See Art Elements in the Contents and Index.

The subject matter — the theme or starting point — may come from observation, from the imagination, or from a mixture of both — like Salvador Dali and the **Surrealists.**

Suggested Assignment

Find out about the Surrealists. (See page 12.)

L'eureux donateur, René Magritte (1898–1967).

The Christ of St John of the Cross, Salvador Dali (1904–1989). Glasgow Art Gallery.

Observe and Discuss

The paintings of Jackson Pollock (1912–56) seem to explode, though he uses no recognisable images.

What do you think of Pollock's painting on page 89?

An approach to painting

There are many things to consider when painting a picture.

- **subject matter** (theme or starting point)
- **composition**
- **colour** (light and shade)
- **technique**
- **materials**

Signposts

See Colour, pages 16–42.
See Tone, page 28.

You may wish to treat your subject matter in a realistic way or an abstract way. Why not experiment with both approaches?

It may be difficult to decide on the treatment of the theme of your picture. It might help to do the following, whether your approach is **realistic** or **abstract.**

Make a list of what might be included in the picture. For a theme such as 'Woodlands', the list might look like this.

Realistic — *emphasis on subject matter*

wood	trees	bark (texture)
leaves (pattern)	cones	twigs
snails	birds	ferns
woodcutter	axe	cabin

Abstract — *emphasis on art elements* (line, colour, texture, pattern, shape and form)

cones (mathematical patterns)		colour of leaves
trees	twigs	wild flowers
cut wood	ferns	rubbish

Doing field work for the 'Woodlands' theme.

Some woodland objects collected during field work.

A realistic treatment of a snail shell.

An abstract treatment of a snail shell.

Signpost

See Art Elements in the Contents and Index.

153

Composition

Once you have made a list of what could be included in your painting, you may then choose some of the possibilities you have listed. Once the problem of what to put in the picture has been solved, the next stage is arrangement or composition.

Composition involves arranging things in a pleasing and balanced way. Any picture, or any surface design, whether realistic or abstract, should use the skill of composition. The aim of a good composition is to keep the viewers' attention, leading them into and around the picture or design.

A few basic points

When beginning a realistic picture, remember that its composition can have three elements.

- foreground
- midground
- background

Observe and Discuss

Study any of the fine art paintings in this book. Can you see a foreground, a midground and a background? Are there any that do not contain these features?

Identify the foreground, midground and background in this student's painting.

Pictorial composition — picture making

Vertical lines give us a feeling of movement. **Horizontal lines** give us a calm, peaceful feeling. These effects are demonstrated in these students' paintings.

Signpost

See Line, pages 70, 163.

Colours are always strongest in the foreground. Because of the atmosphere, colours fade as they go into the distance.

Signpost

See Colour, page 40.

The relationship of composition to emotional response

The three-part guide of foreground, midground and background usually applies to paintings which are realistic. Composition can be much more difficult to define when applied to abstract pictures or designs.

Sometimes we compose a picture out of our imaginations. We might also decide to paint exactly what is in front of us.

Suggested Assignments

1. Select a place or scene which you like. With the aid of your fingers, form a frame around the scene. This will help you define your scene.
2. Make a simple viewfinder with black paper and cut out the required shape.

Signpost

See viewfinder, page 106.

3. For another approach, ignore the viewfinder and arrange your own composition. This may be more difficult, but it allows endless choices.

Students' compositions for both realistic and abstract work.

Painting techniques

All artists develop their own techniques and styles. But everyone must begin by experiencing the actual process of painting.

When painting for the first time, try to experiment with different techniques. When you have done so, you will begin to discover what suits you best. With experience, your own style should emerge.

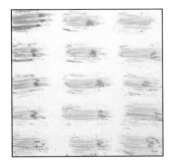

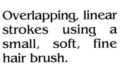

Movement using a solid colour and textured brush strokes in a curving manner.

Overlapping, linear strokes using a small, soft, fine hair brush.

Spatter painting on a wash background using three contrasting colours.

Overlapping, horizontal strokes using a soft brush.

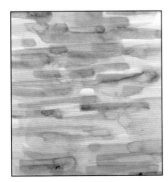

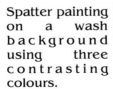

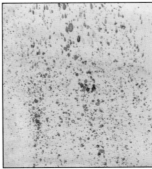

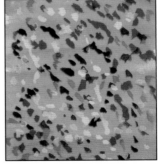

Wash with dabs of colour, using a pointillist technique.

The focal point

The **focal point** is what pulls the viewer into the picture. It is the 'centre of attention' — even though it is not always in the centre.

For most pictures, one should try not to put the focal point right in the middle of the sheet of paper. This tends to divide the picture in two.

People and things should face into your picture to keep the interest going.

A picture divided into two by a central focal point.

Different types of composition

Pictorial balance

Sometimes, it can be possible to place the focal point in the centre. If the middle object is balanced by other things in the scene, the composition may work well.

In da Vinci's painting, *The Last Supper*, Jesus is the central figure, the focal point. He is central to the story and so is well-placed in the middle. The painting uses perspective to bring the viewer's eyes directly to the head of Jesus. This is an excellent example of successful **symmetrical composition**. (See page 157.)

Some pictures are deliberately composed in an off-centre way — these use **asymmetrical composition**. Asymmetrical pictures can also be pleasing to the eye. They tend to hold our attention for much longer.

Which looks more interesting: a picture with a figure going *into* the frame, or with the figure going *out of* the frame?

Observe and Discuss

Look at the linear compositions on page 163. Find the focal point in each composition. A few of these can be quite challenging!

Observe and Discuss

1. Many of Edgar Degas' (1834 –1917) paintings used asymmetrical composition.
2. Look at some paintings by John Constable (1776 –1837), especially *The Haywain*. Discuss Constable's approach to composition.

The Tribute Money, Masaccio (1401–1428). Fresco. Brancacci Chapel, Florence.

The Last Supper, Leonardo da Vinci (1452–1519). Fresco. Milan.

Observe and Discuss

. . . the composition of these two paintings.

The Golden Section

The human eye and brain work together. Things that are appealing to the eye have a sense of balance. Many artists — in painting, sculpture and architecture — have tried to achieve this balance. They decided on their proportions or balance by using the **golden section**.

The golden section refers to a mathematical division or measurement regularly found in Nature. It was first noticed by Euclid, the Father of Modern Geometry, around 300 BC. Such a series is called the *Fibonacci numbers* or Ø ('fie').

1, 1, 2, 3, 5, 8, 13, 21, 34, 55
2 + 3 = 5, 3 + 5 = 8, 5 + 8 = 13 and so on.

Each number is the sum of the previous two.

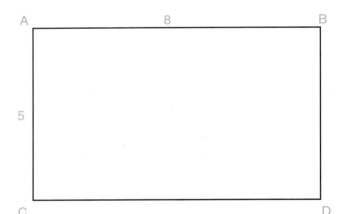

This is a rough golden section rectangle ABCD. It is divided in the proportions of 8 : 13.

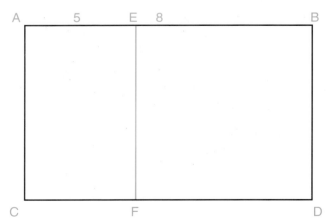

This will reproduce another golden section rectangle AECF standing on its head.

Another easy way to compose your picture is to **divide it into thirds,** both horizontally and vertically. Any of the X points could be the focal point, where the main interest could lie.

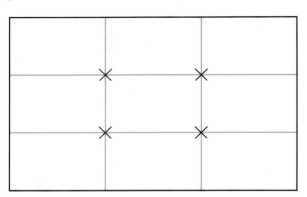

Nature achieves its own balance, as this sunflower shows.

Observe and Discuss

Look at other paintings — both in this book and in other books — to see how the balance has been achieved.

Suggested Assignment

Make up your own compositions based on:
- the golden section
- division in thirds.

When Giotto painted *The Deposition of Christ* he had to trust his own eyes. He was not aware of the mathematical way of working out the golden section. Yet he painted a perfectly balanced picture in which the dead Christ was the main point of interest.

Piero della Francesca (*c.*1410–1492) used the golden section formula when composing his picture, *The Flagellation of Christ*.

Observe and Discuss

. . . the ways in which the following affect compositions.

- proportion   • scale
- perspective   • depth
- overlap   • colour
- light and shade

Signposts

See chapters on Drawing and the other Art Elements. Refer to the Table of Contents and the Index.
See Giotto, page 138.

The Deposition of Christ,
Giotto (1266–1337). Fresco.
Arena Chapèl, Padua.

The Flagellation of Christ,
Piero della Francesca
(c.1410–1492). Panel. Palace
of the Duke, Urbino.

Support Studies

Fantasy and distortion

Even when a picture is abstract, the artist must consider some composition rules. Otherwise the work may not be successful.

In one way, abstract pictures are more difficult to create and compose than realistic ones. Abstract paintings are not mere records but images which may be created totally out of the painter's mind.

Finding a balanced, realistic image is not too difficult when using the viewfinder. But trying to create the same thing from unrecognisable shapes makes this kind of painting very challenging.

To deliberately distort or ignore scale means that you are entering the realms of fantasy. This can be done in a realistic manner as well as abstractly.

St Francis in ecstasy, El Greco (1541–1614). National Gallery of Ireland.

Observe and Discuss

. . . the distortion in the El Greco painting.
. . . the work of Gillian Ayres, page 148, and the work of M.C. Escher, pages 132, 140, 161.

Suggested Assignment

Create your own idea of a fantasy image, based on your theme.

Reviewing composition

Composition is the organisation of a picture, whether realistic or abstract. A good composition will direct the viewer's eye into and around the picture. It helps to communicate serenity, movement or unrest, stability, beauty, violence — almost any emotional reaction such as sadness, happiness, rejection or peace.

However, there is more to any picture than just composition. Other aspects of a picture are the way it is painted, the painter's style, the chosen colours, the media used — even the overall texture of the end result. All of these things must be considered when painting a picture.

Signposts

Look at the work of René Magritte (page 152) and Salvador Dali (pages 12, 152).

See Graphic Design, page 188.

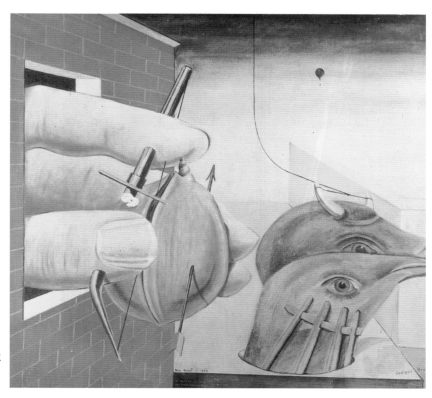

Oedipus Rex, Max Ernst (1891–1976). Claude Herrant, Paris.

Waterfall, M.C. Escher (1898–1972). Lithograph. ©1961 M.C. Escher Foundation, Baarn, Holland

Over the Town, Marc Chagall (1887–1985). Tretjakoff-Galerie, Moscow.

Different compositions — Students' work

Two compositions entitled *After Bridget Riley.*

The Wind.

Signpost

See Bridget Riley, pages 65, 287.

The Relationship of Composition to Emotional Response

Angles = agitation.

Rays attract attention.

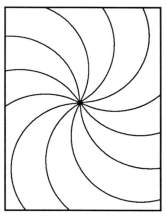

Spirals = excitement.

Triangle = security.

Swirls = movement.

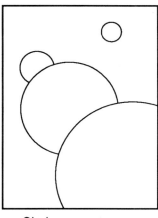

Circles = vastness.

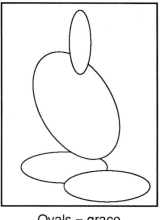

Ovals = grace.

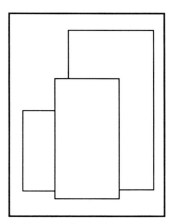

Rectangles = strength.

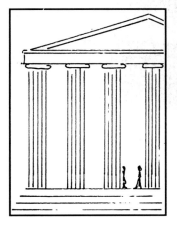

Verticals = stability.

Light = hope.

Horizontals = tranquility.

Radii = glory.

Collage

The word **collage** comes from the French word meaning 'paste up'. A collage is an arrangement or composition made up of pieces of torn or cut paper, cloth or other materials. It might include newspapers, bus tickets, labels and many other common items. A collage could be made up of textured materials such as wallpaper, sandpaper or sweet wrappers. These materials may form all or part of a two-dimensional work such as a drawing or a painting.

Signpost

See Texture, page 80.

Collage is popular as a colour composition exercise. Blocks of cut-out, coloured shapes may be arranged and rearranged until the artist is satisfied with the effect of proportion, balance and colour relationships.

A collage usually consists of a backdrop or background onto which cut-out or torn pieces of paper or other materials are put. This means that space is not created by perspective or foreshortening, but by overlapping and intertwining the layers of collage material.

A student's collage on the theme 'Containers'.

Signposts

See Picasso, page 144.
See Cubism, page 144.

Paper Collage, Georges Braque (1882–1963). Paris.

Paper Collage, Pablo Picasso (1881–1973). Paris.

Support Studies

Collage was developed early in the 20th century by the French Cubists. It became very popular as an art form around 1910 when Georges Braque, Juan Gris and Pablo Picasso introduced pieces of paper, oilcloth and wallpaper into their paintings.

Observe and Discuss

Having mastered the art of collage, Picasso returned to painting, but this time in a style which showed the influence of collage. Look at *Three Musicians* and discuss whether you can see the collage influence.

Three Musicians, Pablo Picasso (1881-1973). Oil on canvas. Museum of Modern Art, New York, Mrs Simon Guggenheim Fund.

Paper cut-outs

In the 1930s, the French artist, Henri Matisse (1869–1954), started using a form of collage which he called 'cut-outs'. He used this device to plan or design his paintings. This allowed him to move figures and other images around on the background before deciding on their final position. In his search for simplification in painting, Matisse found that cut paper was a more direct way of working with shapes and colours.

In his later years, Matisse suffered from ill health and was not able to stand painting at an easel for long periods of time. Since he was confined to a wheelchair, he relied completely on cut-outs.

Apart from being complete pictures in themselves, Matisse also used cut-outs as designs for stained glass windows, decorative tiles, posters and magazine covers.

L'Escargot (The Snail), Henri Matisse (1869–1954). Paper cut-out. Tate Gallery, London.

Signposts

See Matisse, pages 108, 144.
See Collage, page 164.

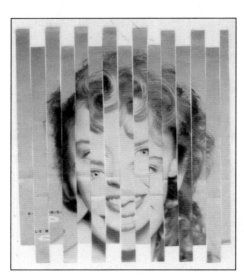

Working with paper.

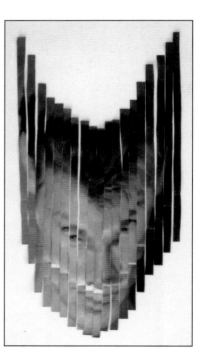

Support Studies

Other methods of using cut paper

• A **montage** is created when images or sections of representational pictures are used to make a new pictorial arrangement.

• A **photomontage** is created when only photographs or printed images are used.

• The **Dada Movement** began in 1916 in Zurich, Switzerland. It consisted of a group of artists who said they were 'anti-art'. They used both collage and montage to produce disturbing effects by distorting conventional images.

• An **assemblage** is created when a construction of 3D objects such as boxes, cardboard, plastics and other materials is grouped together.

Observe and Discuss

Discuss the differences between collage, montage, photomontage and assemblage.

A student's montage.

A student's photomontage.

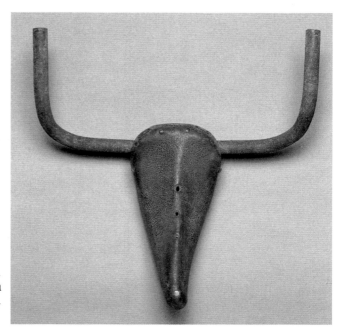

Head of a Bull, Pablo Picasso (1881–1973). An assemblage made of metal tubing and a bicycle seat. Reunion de Musée Nationaux, France.

Suggested Assignment

Create a collage illustrating the theme of Memories/Events — for example, holidays, weddings, special family celebrations.

A collage is an ideal way of arranging some of the souvenirs and keepsakes which are associated with a special event. All these items can be arranged in a pleasing display which will remind those involved of the event at a glance.

Students' collages done for the 'Memories' theme.

Suggested Assignments

Arrange your collages, montages, photomontages and assemblages using your chosen theme as a starting point.

1. Make a collage using only pieces of coloured paper. The cut shapes can be: (a) rectangular and triangular; (b) circular and curved; (c) a combination of (a) and (b).
2. Make a collage with textured material (torn or cut), paper and cloth.
3. Using all or some of the materials mentioned in projects 1 and 2, make another collage. This time, you may paint or draw on it.
4. Make a montage using magazines, calendars, leaflets, photocopied material.
5. Make a photomontage from old (unwanted) photographs. You might also use photographs from newspapers or magazines.
6. Construct a relief assemblage. (A **relief** is a 3-dimensional work which is attached to a flat, 2-dimensional background or support.) Add matchboxes, paper, cardboard and other collected items to your work.
7. Mix up all or part of the above projects and arrange a collage/montage/ photomontage/ assemblage of your own.

Support Studies

A student's work—
the real thing ... and the mosaic

A violet—a natural object.

Mosaic

Mosaic is a technique which uses small pieces of coloured glass or stone to create a picture or a decorative pattern. The glass or stone pieces are called **tesserae**. They are set into a wall or floor using some kind of adhesive.

Mosaics were very common during Greek, Roman and early Christian periods. Old mosaics can be found in Great Britain, the Middle East, Spain and Portugal, Istanbul (e.g. St Sophia), Venice (e.g. St Mark's), in Mexico, even in the ruins of Pompeii in Italy. Very fine examples of early Christian and Byzantine mosaics can be found at Ravenna in Italy.

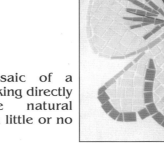

Paper mosaic of a violet (working directly from the natural object with little or no sketching).

Two superb sixth-century mosaics from Ravenna: The Empress Theodora and her court (above) and The Emperor Justinian and his court (right).

The National Autonomous University near Mexico City has a mosaic covering ten storeys of the library building. This mosaic traces the history of Mexico from prehistoric times to the present. It was designed in the 1950s by Juan O'Gorman.

Most artists favour irregular pieces — called **sinnali**. This helps them to scatter light and to create interest in an otherwise flat mosaic. Texture can also be added by including 'mosaic-like' pieces of ceramic (gloss and matt finish).

Support Studies

The mosaic in Dublin's Setanta Centre tells the legend of Cuchulainn. It uses many big ceramic pieces as well as tesserae. This is just a small detail.

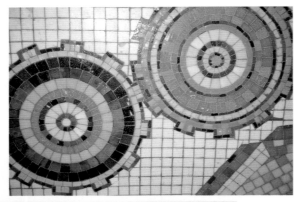

The underground station at Tottenham Court Road in London has been completely transformed with a mosaic by Eduardo Paolozzi. Over 955 square metres of the underground have been covered. Both regular and irregular tesserae were used, as the photographs show.

Mosaics are perfect for public places and are often used to decorate commercial premises. They are durable and easy to clean. They even discourage graffiti. This sheep was an appropiate image for a butcher's shop in Lewisburg, Co. Mayo.

Observe and Discuss

Before creating your own mosaics, look around your area to see if you can find any real mosaics. Churches often contain mosaics. Try to get a photograph of any of the mosaics you find. Find out all you can about the mosaic by interviewing the person in charge. Don't forget that some mosaics are on the ground — like those at the National Museum, National Library and Bewley's Café in Dublin.

Suggested Assignment

Now try your own mosaic. The subject matter is up to you. You may want to use a theme of your own, or one based on a traditional religious or historic scene. It is probably easier to begin by working from a natural or manmade object. Start working with the pieces of coloured paper straight away, rather than working from a drawing or plan.

Support Studies

Making a mural at St Brigid's College, Callan, Co. Kilkenny

Brief: To show the locality (Callan) and its many aspects in a painted collage.

The students first had to go out on location to see and sketch the main points of interest in the town and surrounding locality. Measurements were taken and the mural was drawn to scale using a grid. After all the research and preparations had been completed, the actual painting took approximately six weeks.

Work in progress.

The finished mural.

Printing

November Morning, Maureen Roche. Screen print in 4 colours.

Print making

The earliest known prints were made in China around 150 AD. They were inked rubbings taken from the stone carvings on a tomb.

Woodcuts were being made in China by the eighth century. Rice paper was used to transpose the design to the woodblock. It was then cut out, inked up, and pressed against paper to make a print.

The oldest known printed book is a Buddhist scripture called the *Diamond Sutra*. It was printed with woodcut blocks in China in 868 AD.

A page from the *Diamond Sutra*.

Woodcut prints first appeared in Europe early in the fifteenth century. They were used on playing cards. Before long, woodcuts were being used to make larger religious scenes. The artists Albrecht Dürer and Hans Holbein created superb woodcuts in the sixteenth century.

Signpost

See Albrecht Dürer, pages 88, 105, 132.

It was not until the eighteenth century that **wood engravings** began to appear. A wood engraving is cut from the end grain of a block of boxwood. The art of wood engraving was developed by Thomas Bewick. In the nineteenth century, books and magazines were illustrated with wood engravings.

The Kiss, Edvard Munch (1863–1944). Woodcut printed from two blocks on Japanese paper, Victoria and Albert Museum.

In the late nineteenth century, artists like Munch revived the art of woodcuts. They were attracted by the beautiful textures to be found in wood blocks.

Snipe by Thomas Bewick (1753–1828). Wood engraving, Victoria and Albert Museum.

Bewick's engravings were used in natural history books. They were delicate, detailed and very accurate.

Screen Printing

Samuel Simon of Manchester patented **silk screen printing** in 1907. It was first used for printing fabric in the textile industry, as well as for posters. Today, it has become a very popular artist's medium. Its technical name is **serigraphy**.

Morning Frost, Richard Wardle. Silk screen print. 30 colours. CCA Galleries, London.

La Cathedrale Engloutie, Cathie Felstead. Silk screen print. 10 colours. CCA Galleries, London.

Linoprints

A **linoprint** is taken from an inked lino block, parts of which have been cut away.

Saffron Walden Church, a linoprint by Edward Bowden (1903–1989). Fine Art Society, London.

Etching

In an **etching**, the grooves on the plate are made by an acid which corrodes and eats into the metal. An **aquatint** is a tone etching that gives a watercolour effect. In **drypoint**, no acid is used, and the lines tend to have a velvety quality.

North

Landscape with three gabled cottages, an etching by Rembrandt (1606–1669). Rijksmuseum, Amsterdam.

East

South

Guernsey Grapevine, an original etching by M. B. Whinney.

West

Michael Fairclough (1940-) is an artist whose work shows the many possibilities of aquatint. The series above is called *Hebridean Suite.* Each image is an etching with aquatint, with 2 plates and 6 colours.

Le Trepied Dolmen, an original colour aquatint by Barry Owen Jones.

Young Woman, Paul Cesar Helen (1859–1927). A drypoint etching. Victoria and Albert Museum.

A **lithograph** is made with greasy ink on an absorbent stone which is washed with water. The water repels the printing ink, and the design is printed from the greasy area.

Sheep and Lamb 1974, Henry Moore (1898–1986). A lithograph made with 3 plates and 3 colours. The Henry Moore Foundation.

Zebra , Bryan Organ (1935–).
A lithograph made with 5 plates
and 5 colours.

Observe and Discuss

Prints made from woodcuts, engravings, silk screens, etchings, lithographs and lino blocks are easily recognisable, as each craft has its own distinctive quality.

What effects are created by these printing methods? What work do you appreciate most/ least — and why?

Suggested Assignment

Find examples of different types of prints. Refer to the following artists:

woodcuts and wood engraving — Dürer, Holbein, Thomas Bewick, Eric Gill
etching — Dürer, Rembrandt, Van Dyck, Whistler
aquatint — Goya, Picasso, John Piper
lithograph — Delacroix, Daumier, Toulouse-Lautrec, Whistler

Make a class display of your examples.

Support Studies

Basic printing

A **print** is a mark or image which is usually obtained from a surface that has been coated with some kind of liquid — such as paint or ink. Pressure is then applied to the paper or fabric to reveal the print.

Before you begin to print patterns, you should first make prints from groups of everyday objects. To do this, make a collection of anything that interests you. Then, using a flat bristle brush and thick paint, coat one surface of the object. Then press the inked side onto a sheet of paper to form the print.

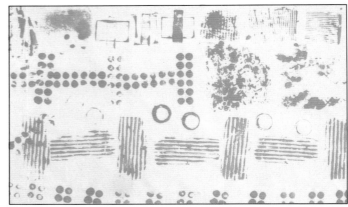

A simple example of printing using everyday objects.

Leaf prints made by students

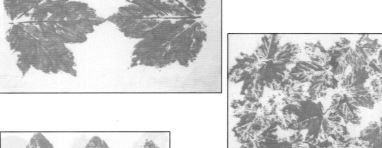

Random pattern.

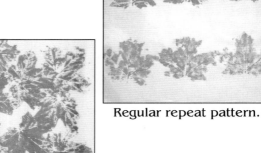

Regular repeat pattern.

Regular repeat pattern.

Repeat pattern using the leaf as a stencil.

2-colour print of a leaf.

Suggested Assignment

Make some simple prints of your own. Then display the results in class. **Observe and discuss** what you have done.

Printing bed

Before starting any form of printing, you will need to make a **printing bed** to reduce the hardness of the work surface. This can simply be an old flat newspaper placed on a table. A printing bed like this is ideal for potato and stencil prints.

For fabric printing, an old blanket, placed on a flat surface and covered with clean newsprint, makes a simple printing bed.

The corner of a detergent box will make an ideal rest for brushes. This stops them from rolling over onto your work.

Potato prints

A simple potato print using a repeat pattern.

When starting potato printing, set aside an area for cutting the potato. Cover this area with newspaper. This will make cleaning up much easier. An old blunt kitchen knife is ideal for cutting the potato. Always cut the potato in one even cut. Otherwise the printing surface will not be flat. Place the cut potato face downwards on newsprint. This will allow the excess moisture to be absorbed.

When applying ink/paint to the potato surface, always ink from one direction only. Re-ink after each print is made. Don't be tempted to make two prints from one inking, as the second print will be much lighter.

If you plan on using a potato to make repeat pattern prints, then mark the back of the potato to ensure that it will always be turned in the same direction. A small cut-away V will give you the right direction.

179

Potato Printed Patterns

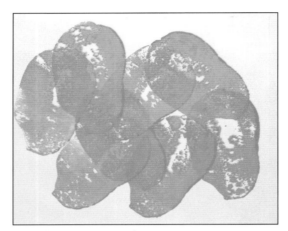

Random potato print.

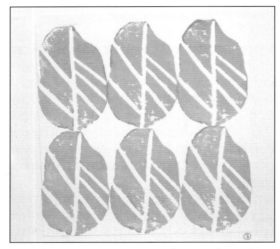

Regular repeat pattern using straight lines.

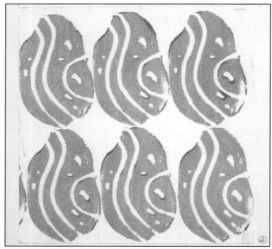

Regular repeat pattern using curved lines plus texture.

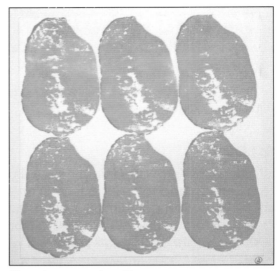

Regular repeat pattern.

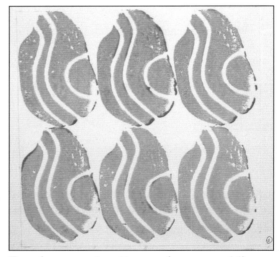

Regular repeat pattern using curved lines.

Using a square-shaped potato block and printing a regular repeat pattern from it.

This chequerboard pattern was made using first a tint and then a shade on the one block.

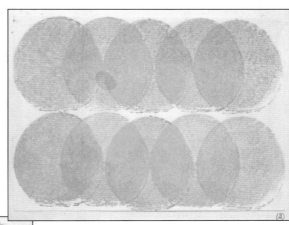

Simple overlapping pattern (using the natural shape of the potato).

A half-drop overlapping pattern using the natural potato shape with curved lines.

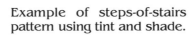

Example of steps-of-stairs pattern using tint and shade.

Examples of students' potato prints on fabric.

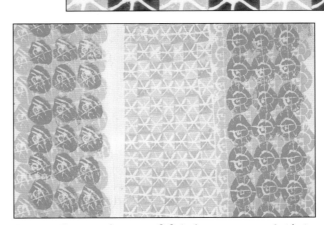

Later, these pieces of fabric were made into individual toilet bags by the students.

A group of students showing their attempts at potato printing on fabric. Although similar in some ways, each pattern is as unique as the person who made it.

A selection of the toilet bags made by these students.

Potato blocks based on geometric shapes

Introducing the diamond

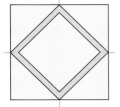

Strike mid-points first at the sides of the potato. Then cut across the potato.

Two-colour printing

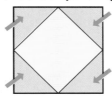 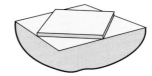

Ink up the corners of the potato print. When the surface is printed, cut away the corners by lowering the surface. Then commence with the diamond.

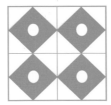  

This is an example of the results achieved from two colour printing.

 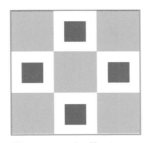  

a regular repeat

Chequered effect using two blocks

Regular repeat of two colours using one block

1. 2. centre cut away

This pattern was created using these two blocks.

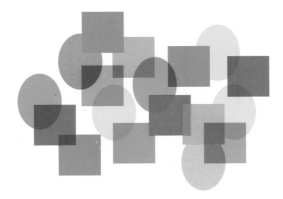

two blocks using several colours and experimenting with transparencies in colour

Some diamond patterns created by students.

Other geometric shapes

Always use a rectangular or square format.

Basic techniques

The octagon
1. Cut a potato in half.
2. Form into a square. Mark each side of the potato in thirds.
3. Cut away at an angle between each corner mark.
4. Surface decorations can be line, texture or cut-away shapes.

The arch
The arch originated in Persia (now Iran). It was used for domes of mosques and is sometimes called 'onion shaped' (ogee).
1. Form a diamond.
2. Bisect the edges and inner diamond.
3. To create the curve, follow the diagram.

Oval shapes

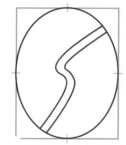 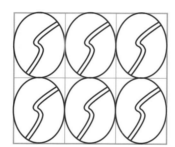

Signpost

See page 179.

Suggested Assignments

1. Make random patterns and simple repeat patterns using both leaves and potatoes. Experiment with different kinds of coloured paper.
2. Try some prints using the geometric shapes described here.

Octagon pattern.

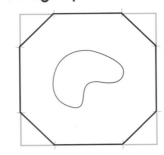 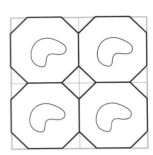

The arch (ogee)

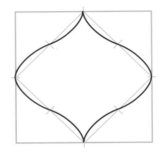 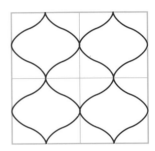

Variations on oval shapes

 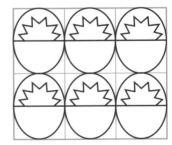

Variations in printing

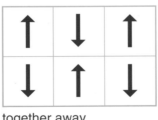

together away
away together

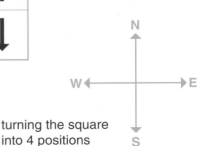

turning the square
into 4 positions

Mono prints

A **monoprint** is a single print. The basic reason for making a monoprint is to experience the transferring or *offsetting* of an image from an inked surface to paper. It is totally unlike a painting made directly onto paper.

A simple monoprint can be made like this.
1. Ink or paint up a flat piece of glass.
2. Create a line drawing in the ink using any drawing tool — including your finger.
3. Place a clear sheet of paper over this. Use the side of your hand in a circular motion to apply even pressure over the entire surface.
4. Peel the paper off, starting with one corner.

Here is a second type of monoprint.
1. Apply an even coat of paint or ink to a sheet of glass.
2. Gently place a sheet of paper over the inked surface. Be careful not to apply any pressure with your fingers.
3. On the back of your paper, draw an image using a rounded point, such as the handle of a paint brush. The finer the point, the narrower will be the line created.
4. Gently peel away the paper from the inked surface.

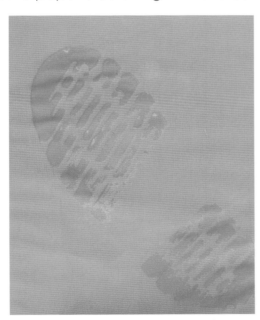

The Blue Shoe, a student's simple monoprint.

This cartoon character was done by a student using the second method.

A finger drawing of a tree was used in the making of this print.

Suggested Assignment

Try making some simple monoprints of your own by following these instructions.

Simple stencil prints

Stencilling originated in China in the eighth century AD. It is believed that fine strands of human hair or silk were used to hold the stencil together.

Signpost

See Screen Printing, page 174.

A stencilled border.

Stencils can also be made by folding the paper in half, then in quarters, then diagonally.

Items required for stencil printing
paper for stencil
knife
printing paper
brush
printing bed
paint
sponge

A simple stencil can be made by cutting a shape out of paper.
1. The simplest way is to fold a sheet of paper in half.
2. Using scissors, cut out an abstract shape
3. Flatten out the stencil and place it on top of a clean sheet of paper.
4. Use a sponge to apply the paint evenly over the stencil surface.
5. Lift the stencil carefully to reveal a print of the cut-out shape.

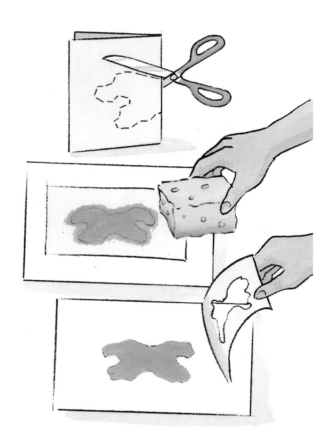

Support Studies

Stencils are ideal for decorating large surfaces such as walls, floors or furniture. Stencilling was the usual method of decorating walls until wallpaper became cheaply available at the end of the nineteenth century.

Any drawing can be simplified for stencil printing. The following example includes a chocolate bar and a scissors. It was cut using a craft knife. Use a sharp blade to get clear, precise edges. Always cut out on a cutting board.

Students working on stencils in class

Here are some stencil prints of plants using 3 colours.

Suggested Assignments

Using your chosen theme, make and execute a stencil print in 3 colours.

Graphic Design

These examples show that we are surrounded by graphic design. Comment on the variety and the styles.

Support Studies

The main function of **graphic design** is to convey a message in a striking manner. Graphic design deals with the more commercial side of art — advertising, printing, promotional work. It can include symbols, lettering, shop fronts, logos, signs, posters, billboards, record covers, CD, cassette and video covers, stamp design, book jackets and covers, book illustrations and book layout. Graphic art is used in books, magazines, newspapers, brochures, menus, invitations, catalogues, tickets and packaging. Graphics are also used in films, videos and animation.

Graphic design is two-dimensional. This two-dimensional work is normally applied by printing or painting on a flat surface, such as paper, card or board, which is then made into packages, boxes or containers. It can also be printed on a three-dimensional structure such as bottles.

The message to be conveyed in graphic design can involve visual images, lettering, or a combination of both.

Colour

Many graphics are in black and white. But colour is also of great importance in graphic design. A good knowledge of colour is essential for graphic designers. It helps them to decide on which colour combination will give the greatest impact or which best suits the design project they are working on.

Image only

Lettering only

PUT YOUR

LITTER

IN THE

BIN

Combination of image and lettering

Signpost

See Graphic Designers, page 239.

Support Studies

Images, signs and symbols

An **image** is something visual. It can be any picture, illustration, photograph, design, sign or symbol.

A **sign** is any mark used to represent or point out something — such as the male and female signs on toilet doors.

A **symbol** is something which stands for or represents an idea.
- **The lion** is the symbol of courage.
- **The dove** is the symbol of peace.
- **A red cross** is the symbol for medical aid.

In graphic design, images are reduced to signs. A sign can be a minimal image with just enough detail for the object to be recognised without being an accurate picture. Signs can be 'read', like an international language. Even people who cannot read can read signs. Signs are particularly important in places such as airports, where people of many languages may gather. They are also important at international meetings such as the Olympic Games.

Suggested Assignments

Make a collection of signs and symbols.

Observe and Discuss

What makes a successful sign or symbol? Were any of those which you collected difficult to interpret? Did the people in your group differ in their interpretations?

The human face

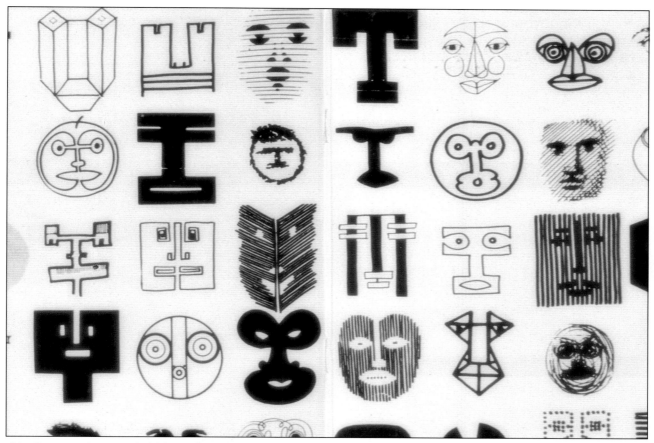

Studies on the possibilities of recognising the human face, Bruno Munari, Israel Museum.

Observe and Discuss

. . . the faces shown here.

Suggested Assignment

Design a graphic face of your own.

Support Studies

Lettering

When lettering/words alone are used, the style of lettering, the layout and the spacing are of great importance.

There is usually no need to attract the person's attention to these graphics. They are normally delivered by hand or by post and viewed close-up. Such examples of graphic design can be seen on invitations, bills, business stationery, advertising leaflets etc.

Note the 'decorative' lettering.

Sometimes lettering can be used in such a creative way that the lettering itself becomes the image.

A student's creative use of lettering for the word 'spray'. Try doing this with words like 'drop', 'kick', 'eye', 'race'—there are many possibilities!

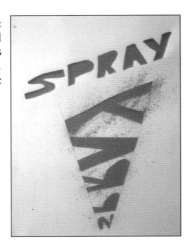

Special lettering can also be used as the **trademark** or **logo** for a well-known product.

The **Mars** logo with its distinctive lettering, but without colour.

The designer's specifications for colour.

The finished **Mars** logo, incorporating lettering and colour.

Signposts

See Alphabets and Letters, page 196.
See Logos and Logotypes, pages 211-212.

Images and lettering

Most graphic design involves both an image and lettering/words.

Nearly everything today is labelled in some way. Whether it is a product, a place, a firm or a concert tour, it will have a label or a name, as these posters show.

Things are given labels to make them immediately recognisable. This leads us into the world of advertising. Here, the image and the lettering must complement each other as they try to communicate with the viewer and create the maximum impact.

The image in this Guinness poster is so powerful and familiar that the product is not even named!

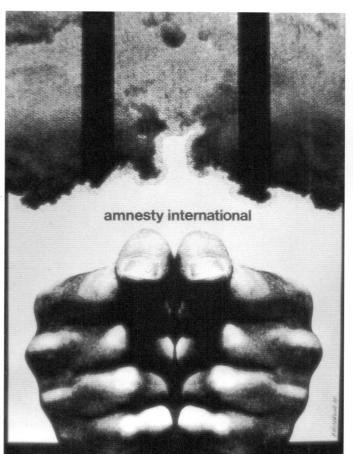

Using small, bold lettering, this Amnesty International poster has a powerful image.

U2 posters always use recognisable lettering.

Observe and Discuss

. . . the images and the lettering on these posters.

Suggested Assignment

Start collecting examples of any images, signs and lettering that you like. Why do you like the things you have collected? Did many people in your group select the same things?

Support Studies

Signs

Road signs

We often think of road signs as using lettering only.

This may be true for many road signs — those which show the distance and direction to a certain place. But road signs also give information by their:
- shape
- colour
- images

Shape

In Ireland, **warning signs** are diamond-shaped.

Signs giving orders come in triangular, circular and octagonal shapes.

Colour

Warning signs have black images on a yellow background.

Signs giving orders normally use black on a white or red background.

Traffic light colours are symbols themselves.

Signpost

See Colour, page 40.

Other signs

The arrow is a well-known directional sign.

With increasing travel, more and more road signs and symbols are being standardised in many countries.

Observe and Discuss

. . . these international signs. Are there any signs which you find confusing? Could you create a better sign?

Suggested Assignments

1. Design a graphic (without using words) to direct motorists to a sports centre.
2. Design a road sign warning motorists that there is a danger of flooding ahead.
3. Design a road sign directing motorists to an agricultural/farm show or a ploughing championship.

Support Studies

Letters and Alphabets

Letters are the building blocks of the written language. They are abstract shapes which have a meaning. When letters are put together in the correct order, they form words. And words are used to communicate information.

Writing was invented when early civilisations learned how to communicate in a non-verbal way. Later on, the alphabet was developed from stylised pictures, such as those seen on Egyptian tombs.

These stylised pictures gradually became more and more simplified. They ended up as those symbolic marks which we call letters.

A Phoenician inscription carved in stone, 5th century BC.

Hieroglyphics from an Egyptian tomb at Karnac used stylised pictures instead of letters.

This Greek inscription, also from the 5th century BC, uses letters similar to ours.

Support Studies

The History of the Alphabet

The word **alphabet** comes from the first two letters in the Greek alphabet, *alpha* and *beta*. The Greek alphabet is an adaptation of the earlier Phoenician alphabet. The Phoenicians were a people who lived along the coast of the Mediterranean in pre-Christian times. Their alphabet dates from around 1000 BC.

The Romans used both Greek and Phoenician alphabets as the basis for their own. They added extra symbols and formed the Roman alphabet. It consisted of 23 letters and looked much the same as our capital letters today.

The Roman alphabet formed the basis of our modern alphabet. It was often cut into stone. The most beautiful of these carved inscriptions is the one at the base of Trajan's Column in Rome.

Trajan's Column (113 AD) and the inscription at its base. A large portion of the Roman population could read and write at this time.

Majuscule and miniscule

An alternative alphabet with small letters did not begin to appear until around the end of the eighth century. This style was called **Carolingian miniscule**.

Majuscule and **miniscule** writing can be found in old Irish **manuscripts** (a manuscript is any book or document written by hand).

Majuscule script is written between two horizontal lines.

Miniscule script is written between four lines, with the main body of the lettering contained between the two inner lines.

Irish majuscule is in fact a form of writing in round capitals. Irish manuscripts were written in Latin using a Gaelic script.

A page from the *Book of Kells* (late 8th century AD) telling about the Last Supper and the First Eucharist. This beautiful book can be seen in the Library of Trinity College, Dublin.

Part of the Gospel of St Luke from the *Book of Kells,* written in majuscule script.

A page from the Stowel Missal, written in miniscule script. Royal Irish Academy, Dublin.

Support Studies

Eastern writing

The Chinese and Japanese have no alphabets. Their written communication consists of thousands of characters, rather than 26 letters. Most of these characters are based on **pictorial symbols**. In the East, brushes instead of pens or pencils have been used for thousands of years to produce beautiful **calligraphy**.

Observe and Discuss

. . . the development of lettering. It is interesting to look at different lettering systems, both past and present.

In Chinese, each character is a single word. Chinese is read vertically, and from right to left. In China, fine handwriting is seen as a mark of respect. This is especially true for religious work, like this one about the Buddha from the 10th century AD.

During the Middle Ages, monks painstakingly copied manuscripts by hand. They decorated the pages with intricate colourful images. The initial letter on each page was given special attention. This is called **illumination** (illumination means illustration or decoration).

By the fifteenth century, an alphabet of small letters (**lower case**) and large or capital letters (**upper case**) had developed in Western Europe.

The terms 'lower case' and 'upper case' come from the positions of the drawers on a printer's desk. The **lower case (small) letters** were stored in the bottom drawers — the lower case. The **upper case (capital) letters** were stored in the top drawers — the upper case.

This elaborate Chi Rho page is a fine example of illumination from *The Book of Kells.* It is still as clear and beautiful now as it was when it was created over 1000 years ago.

AaBbCcDdEe
FfGgHhIiJjKk
LlMmNnOoPp
QqRrSsTtUu
VvWwXxYyZz

Interesting alphabets

During the 19th century, there was a renewed interest in lettering. Some old alphabet designs were revived. Many were modernised and others were invented.

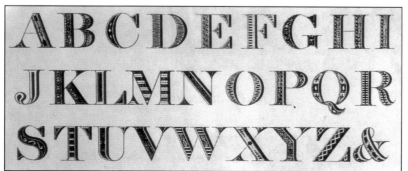

Support Studies

Johann Gutenberg (c.1400 – 68) invented the printing press around 1450. The widespread use of the printing press standardised lettering. It made words and writing available to a greater number of people.

Gutenberg's printing press.

The first book printed by Gutenberg was the Holy Bible.

Suggested Assignments

1. Collect examples of writing from around the world.
2. Design your own illuminated initials, based on what you see in illuminated manuscripts.
3. Try to develop your own personal alphabet, based on those shown in this book.

Observe and Discuss

. . .any differences and similarities between this page from Gutenberg's Bible and the page from *The Book of Kells* on page 197.

Support Studies

Calligraphy

The word **calligraphy** comes from two Greek words which mean 'beautiful writing'. Calligraphy was a skill practised in former times when it was considered part of a complete education. Even today, in this technological age, there has been an increased interest in calligraphy. Many people appreciate and value what is done completely by hand. Calligraphy adds a personal touch and is much sought after for special inscriptions on such things as birth certificates and wedding albums.

abcdefghij
klmnopqrs
tuvwxyz

Italic writing

In Italy during the fifteenth century, new styles of writing were developed. One of these was *italic writing*, in which all the letters are slanted forward. It is now a very popular style of calligraphy and is quick enough to be used in everyday writing.

abcdefghij
klmnopqrs
tuvwxyz

The computer age

Computers and word processors can produce almost any **typeface** (style of lettering), depending on the computer program. People can do page layouts on computers, and special software provides a huge variety of sizes and styles. Some programs can take away the drudgery of centring and measuring up lettering. They do have their limitations when it comes to creativity. But a skilful combination of computers and one's own work could give exciting results by a fusing of art and technology.

A modern word processor, with its keyboard and printer.

Plain Plain Plain Plain Plain Plain Plain Plain Plain Plain
Bold Bold Bold Bold Bold Bold Bold Bold
Italic Italic Italic Italic Italic Italic Italic
Bold Bold Bold Bold Bold Bold Bold
Italic Italic Italic Italic Italic Italic Italic
Plain Plain Plain Plain Plain Plain
Bold Bold Bold Bold Bold Bold Bold
Italic Italic Italic Italic Italic Italic

A computer print-out using a variety of sizes and typefaces.

Suggested Assignment

Try writing your own name in a special script style — as you might like to see it written on an award certificate.

Support Studies

Working with lettering

Good lettering is a basic part of graphic design. Everyone is familiar with letters, of course. But few people take the time to look at the many different shapes, styles and sizes of letters which are used today.

An amazing selection of Gs used in the design of a German calendar.

Observe and Discuss

The first thing to do when studying lettering is to pick a commonly used word. Then, look in newspapers and magazines to see how many different ways this word is written.

Suggested Assignments

Cut out examples of your chosen word and assemble them at random on a sheet of paper. Now study the different approaches to the word. Make a note of them under the following headings.
- size
- style
- weight (heavy/fat, light/thin)
- colour
- shading and background
- position (spacing)

What did these students discover when working with 'the' and 'new'?

What letters say

Letters say alot about a word. The size, style, weight, colour and position are all very important when trying to create a certain image.

Look at these examples of the lettering for a bank. Just from looking at the lettering, where do you think most people would choose to open an account? Few people would choose the bank on the top. They would not take such lettering seriously, and banking is a serious business. Though plain and simple, the bank using the lettering on the bottom is the one that would inspire confidence and a feeling of stability.

Look at business premises or shop fronts in your local area. See whether the lettering style reflects or relates to the business operation. Was any style particularly good? Did you find any styles which you thought were inappropriate?

Practical lettering

To master the art of lettering, students should first try a simple form. This can act as a starting point for the development of creative lettering.

This practical lettering assumes that all letters are the same width (except for 'I'). It ignores the fact that M and W usually need more space and that Q is a little longer than the average letter. Letters usually look better when the height is greater than the width.

This style of lettering can be drawn. It can also be cut out from paper, card or potato. Place the cut-out letters on a poster or create the design for a book jacket or video cover. Then move the letters around until the space is just right. This should save alot of time and keep the finished work clean.

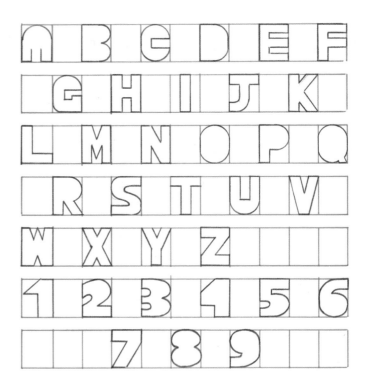

A block alphabet with curves and straight lines. The curves give the alphabet a less stiff appearance. It assumes that all letters are the same width.

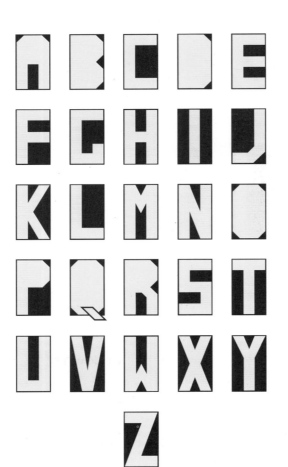

This block alphabet is made with straight lines only. It is suitable for stencil work.

Suggested Assignments

Experiment with cutting out your own alphabet, using straight lines only. Do this sentence, taking layout and spacing into account.

The quick brown fox jumps over the lazy dog.

Cut out an alphabet using both straight lines and curves.

Formal block lettering

The more formal type of lettering needs a **grid**. A grid is a series of horizontal and vertical guidelines, as used on graph paper. The size of the grid that is used depends on the size of lettering required.

When one is starting off, the best grid is one which is in units of 1cm x 1cm, as shown on page 206.

The rule is simple. All letters take 3 units across and 5 units down, with a few exceptions.

I	=	1 unit across and 5 down
M	=	4 units across and 5 down
W	=	5 units across and 5 down

A, H, N = 3 units across and 5 down
M, W   = 4 units across and 5 down

Learn one size for each of these letters and stick to it!

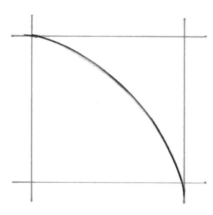

Where natural curves occur, confine the curves to the box.

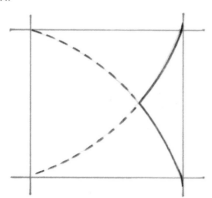

Watch for the middle section of the B.

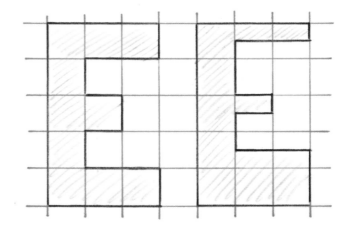

The thickness of the lines within the letter is *usually* the thickness of the unit. Of course, this may be changed if a special effect is required.

Letter shapes and groups

Letter shapes may be broken into various groups.

- **Straight-lined letters**
  A, E, F, H, I, K, L, M, N, T, V, W, X, Y, Z
- **Circular letters**
  C, G, O, Q
- **Curved and straight**
  B, D, J, P, R, S, U

There is another approach to grouping letters.

V is like an upside-down A, without the horizontal stroke.
W is like a double V.
E is like a B linked up on the right side.
F is like an E without the bottom stroke.
D is like an O with one straight side.
Q is like an O with a stroke.
G is like a C with an extra stroke.
P is like an R without the final down stroke.

Suggested Assignment

Do a block lettering alphabet. The sample on page 206 will help you.

205

A Sample Block Alphabet

Letter spacing

It is fairly easy to space the examples of block lettering on pages 204-206. These letters take more or less the same space, except for A.

If A is put beside T, V, W or Y, it must get closer to these letters. Otherwise the letter spacing will look too open.

AT   AT

AVAIL   AVAIL

AWAY   AWAY

Other lettering styles may require more adjusting of the letter spacing. For example, if an O is put beside another O, or a rounded letter such as C, G or Q, the letters will have to be moved closer together.

LOOK   LOOK

The same goes for T, V, W and Y when placed beside a round letter.

TOE   TOE

OVER   OVER

WOOD   WOOD

YOGHURT   YOGHURT

When using a style of lettering that includes pointed as well as rounded letters — A, V, W, C, G, O, Q — it may be necessary to let these extend slightly above and below the grid. This will preserve the illusion that all the letters in that style are of the same size.

GLOVE

AROMA

WAG

QUICK

WOOL

VAN

Suggested Assignments

1. Write these words in block lettering with special reference to spacing.

DANCE	FAIR	FASHION	CIRCUS
VARIETY	VARY	ATTACK	YACHT
TAKE	CLOCK	LAW	YOKE
ZOO	DISCO	DOOR	WORK

2. Write these words in a Roman style lettering.

207

Word spacing and line spacing

Spacing is not limited simply to the space between letters. Other spacings must be considered as well. Otherwise it would be difficult to read what has been written.

ITISHARDTOREADWOR
DSWHENTHEREISNOSP
ACING

Why not try writing a sentence without any word spacing? The result should look something like this. Now put in the spacing and try again.

IT IS HARD TO READ
WORDS WHEN THERE
IS NO SPACING

There are three kinds of spacing involved in lettering.

1. the space between letters
2. the space between words
3. the space between lines

Most of us would not dream of writing without using these three kinds of spacing. But it is surprising how people forget about spacing when they are making a poster, notice or sign.

Suggested Assignment

Write your name and address. Pay particular attention to the spacing between the lines, as well as the spacing between the words.

Support Studies

Transfer lettering
(rub-down lettering such as Letraset)

Everyone should have some knowledge of transfer lettering. It has many advantages and comes ready to use. But unless you have a complete range of styles, you may be tempted to make do with an inappropriate style.

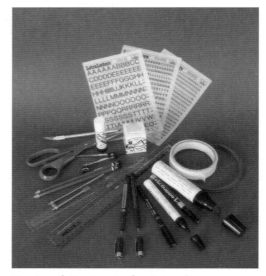

Tools of the trade for lettering.

Spacing becomes very important when using transfer lettering. It is very easy to make transfer lettering look shoddy if incorrect spacing is used.

It is difficult to beat the individuality of your own specially-designed lettering, as this student's work shows.

Support Studies

Once some basic forms of lettering have been learned, it is easy to adapt them in different ways.

Distorted letters are easily achieved by twisting or denting the grid.

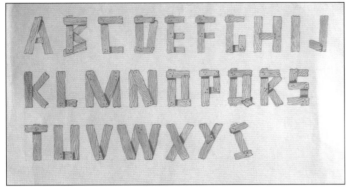

A wooden alphabet would be challenging.

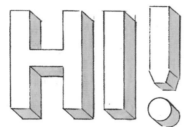

A shadow may be added, giving a solid block like appearance.

Why not try out some descriptive words?

Perspective lettering gives the illusion of 'coming at you'. You can create good effects by pasting perspective lettering over backgrounds from magazines.

Suggested Assignments

1. Try to design your own alphabet. Why not base it on a theme which is of interest to you?
2. Experiment with different techniques, such as stencil-making.

Signpost

See Stencils, page 186.

Support Studies

Designing a special letter

This student gave the letter 'A' a Celtic touch.

Once the design for that special letter has been done, it can then be adapted for different uses. How about a card for someone whose name begins with that letter? It could be put at the beginning of a story or poem. It could be embroidered or screen/stencil printed.

Why stop with one letter? Try to design your own **monogram** using your initials. Some thought should be given to the image your monogram should have. (Remember the 'Bank' example on page 203?)

Students enjoy designing their own monograms.

Some students' monograms kept to the block-like letters. Others developed along a more script-like style with curved lines.

Colours also play an important part in how an image is realised. So choose carefully!

Suggested Assignment

Collect examples of one letter of your choice.

Observe and Discuss

. . . your collection of lettering. Notice how different styles are suitable for:
- cards
- embroidery
- stencil/screen prints
- monograms

Support Studies

Logos

Monograms are sometimes used in business. They are made into the company's logo.

A **logo** — or a trademark — is used by most companies. It is a type of shorthand label. It lets the public know, at a glance, what the company, institution or product is.

A **logo** is an emblem or symbol which usually stands on its own without using letters or words.

A **logotype** is usually an emblem or symbol made up of initials or a word. It may be a single letter or a monogram.

The term 'logo' is often used loosely to describe a combination of both logos and logotypes.

Some Irish logos

Credit Union.

Sculptors' Society of Ireland.

Irish Wildbird Conservancy.

AN BORD IASCAIGH MHARA
IRISH SEA FISHERIES BOARD

211

Some international logos

Mercedes-Benz

CERTIFICATION TRADE MARK

PURE NEW WOOL

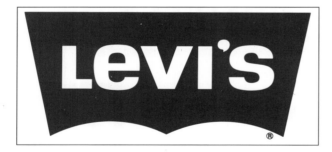

Suggested Assignments

1. Collect a selection of logos (on business cards, in newspapers and magazines).
2. Design a logo for an engineering firm owned by a person named Brennan. Use black and white with one other colour.
3. Design a logo for a shoe factory which specialises in children's footwear. Use black and white combined with two colours.

Observe and Discuss

Pick out one or two logos and say what you think of them and why. Do these logos reflect the business or organisation they represent?

212

Designing a cheese label and logo

Design brief
To design an Irish farmhouse cheese label/logo for Claire Coogan.

Use only two colours. The label must be round, as that is the shape of the cheese. The cheese is yellow/cream in colour, and slightly lighter on the inside. The design must be suitable for use on posters, letter-heads and business cards.

The rough draft of ideas, design, lettering and colour
The 3 'Cs' — Claire Coogan's Cheese — provided a good starting point from which the whole design evolved.

The designer's ideas were presented to the client.

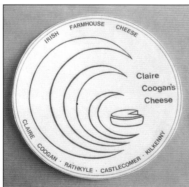

The approved design without colour.

The finished label, with lettering changed by client. Design by Clodagh Holahan.

Radio station logo

Design brief
To design the logo for a radio station called Radio Kilkenny, with a wavelength of 96.6FM.

It should be catchy and memorable. It will be used on billboards, on the mobile broadcasting unit, as the office front, on posters, car stickers, letter-heads, business cards — anything and everything to do with the station.

The overall colour would be red and yellow — not black and amber (the Kilkenny colours), as it might be mistaken for a hurling or football club.

The 'i' in 'radio' became the radio mast, radiating radio waves throughout the design/logo. The idea was liked, although a few minor adjustments had to be made. One colour — red — proved to be stronger and more sophisticated, so the second colour was dropped.

The designer's original ideas.

The final design as used on the company's stationery. Design by Clodagh Holahan.

A Corporate Image

A company's **corporate image** involves a unified design which is used by every possible aspect of the business. Here we see just a few of the ways in which Aer Lingus represents itself.

With Compliments

A 'compliments' slip.

An Aer Lingus check-in desk.

Aer Lingus ❀

The Aer Lingus logo.

Aer Lingus ❀

Dublin Airport, Dublin, Ireland

Telephone: Head Office 01-705 2222
General Fax 01-705 3832
Telegrams/Telex: Dublin 31404

Direct Telephone Number

Direct Fax Number

Aer Lingus stationery.

An Aer Lingus Boeing 747.

Observe and Discuss

. . . these images.
. . . any other ways in which Aer Lingus could use its corporate image.

Support Studies

Traditional shop fronts

The traditional Irish shop front dates from the late 19th or early 20th centuries. The smaller shops had simple, classical columns made of timber. These were usually interpreted according to local tradition.

The lettering and signs involved many variations of classical and other alphabets. These reflected the architectural style of the buildings. Signs could be read without any difficulty.

Shop fronts used strong, bright colours in an uninhibited way. This gave a real character to the whole street.

Display windows were usually small and had a vertical format.

Observe and Discuss

The recent trend in small villages and towns is to restore and redecorate shop fronts in the style of the 19th and early 20th centuries. What do you think of this? Is it successful? Unsuccessful?

A detail from Real Ireland Design's poster, *Irish Shop Fronts.*

Support Studies

Posters

The origin of posters

Posters are more than just public notices. The aim of a public notice is to inform or command. The aim of a poster is to seduce, to inform, to convince, to educate, to appeal or to sell.

Posters have been an important means of visual communication for hundreds of years. The earliest ones were simply handbills or signboards. Around 1870, modern posters began to make a real impact on commerce and art. This was due to the improvements in lithographic printing, along with the creativity of the French artist, Jules Chéret (1836–1933).

Jules Chéret's posters were colourful and full of vitality. This, it is said, was because he drew his designs straight onto the lithographic stone.

Apart from being advertisements, Chéret himself also claimed that posters made good murals. Chéret designed over 1000 posters. Today, they are regarded as works of art.

This poster by Jules Chéret was designed in 1900. It is advertising petrol.

Signpost

See Product Posters, page 223.

Support Studies

Henri de Toulouse-Lautrec

Henri de Toulouse-Lautrec (1864–1901) lived for much of his short life in Montmartre, the entertainment district of Paris. He is famous for his posters and paintings of Parisian nightlife.

Because of injuries he had suffered as a child, Toulouse-Lautrec had a strange dwarf-like appearance. While his body continued to grow, his legs did not develop. This made him extremely sensitive, so he sought the company of other outcasts in society such as prostitutes. In fact, he came from a noble family which was extremely wealthy. But Toulouse-Lautrec preferred the colourful slums of Paris to his family home.

The work of Toulouse-Lautrec was influenced by Japanese print makers and the Post-impressionists, especially Vincent van Gogh (1853–1890) and Paul Gauguin (1848–1903).

He immortalised many famous cabaret artistes in his work, especially women such as Jane Avril, Mary Bedfort, La Goulue and Yvette Guilbert.

Toulouse-Lautrec managed to combine words and images so well that the images 'read' as clearly as the words, which never took over the poster's design. Some of his posters were considered ugly at the time, especially because he often caricatured his subjects. However, his use of dark, flat shapes and foreshortening was striking. His lettering was simple and spontaneous.

In one of his last posters of Jane Avril, Toulouse-Lautrec loses the background 'props' completely. He relies only on his model's image together with her name.

Although he designed only thirty-one posters, Toulouse-Lautrec has left his mark on poster history.

Signpost

See Foreshortening, page 130.

Two more posters designed by Toulouse-Lautrec.

Observe and Discuss

. . . the work of Toulouse-Lautrec.

Support Studies

Today, a large proportion of advertising is done on radio and television. Before this, however, posters were almost the only means of advertising. Posters were and still are very effective means for communicating information about many things — entertainment, products, travel, restaurants. During the two world wars of this century, posters were used extensively for propaganda.

Posters were also very popular with shipping companies and were used in very dramatic ways. Perspective was used to great effect. This exaggerated the size, speed and strength of the vessels.

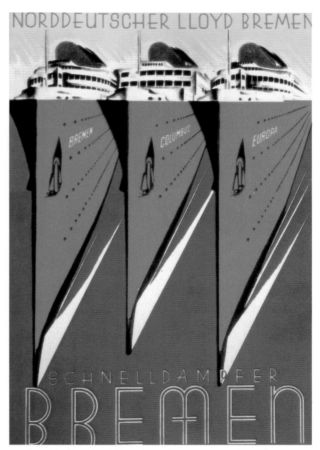

This 1925 poster was used to advertise the 'quick steamers' *Bremen, Columbus* and *Europa*. It uses foreshortening to create a dramatic visual effect.

The Pointing Posters

One very famous poster theme was the pointing finger. It was first used in Great Britain during the First World War. The designer, Alfred Leete, used a man named Lord Kitchener as his model. He is pointing and staring directly at the viewer, almost defying anyone to avoid his glance. This was an extremely powerful image for a successful recruiting campaign for the British army.

The pointing finger catches your attention immediately. It is a frontal attack on the viewer, with a marvellous foreshortening of the arm and hand. It is difficult to turn away from such a poster, as it singles out 'you'. Alfred Leete's poster was so successful that it was copied in various forms by a number of countries both during and after the First World War. Since then, it has been adapted for many uses.

The original pointing poster, designed in 1914 by Alfred Leete and featuring Lord Kitchener. Imperial War Museum.

An American recruitment poster designed in 1917 by James Montgomery Flagg.

A recent poster for the American Marines also used Leete's idea. However, instead of pointing, the Marine is beckoning to the observer.

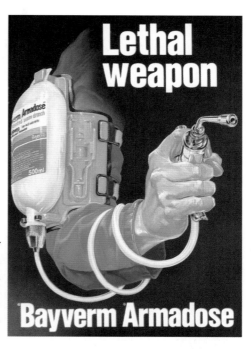

A modern adaptation of Alfred Leete's idea. This time, the product — a worm drench produced by Bayer — replaces the head. The finger is a drench gun.

Support Studies

Transport posters

During the 1920s and '30s, there were many innovations in the world of travel. Well designed posters reflected these developments.

Signpost

See the 'quick steamers' poster, page 219.

A dramatic poster for the P&O shipping company.

Étoile du Nord was designed in 1927 by A. M. Cassandre (1901-1968). Its brilliant use of perspective gives the impression of speed.

221

Moving posters

With so many people on the move—in cars, buses, trains, vans—advertisers have discovered that it pays to move along with them. The 'moving poster' is now seen everywhere we look.

One of the most successful and popular 'moving posters'—the Smarties bus from Dublin Bus Advertising.

Billboards

More than any other type of poster, **billboards** must be easy to read. As they are usually situated on busy roads, they must get their message across quickly and clearly.

Observe and Discuss

. . . the two billboards shown here.
. . . the effectiveness and location of billboards in your area.

Observe and Discuss

. . . the different types of moving posters that you see. Do you think they are effective?

Support Studies

Product Posters

Observe and Discuss

. . . these posters. At what audience are they aimed? Do they make us stop and look? Do they concentrate on words or images? Why?

Support Studies

Some Irish Posters

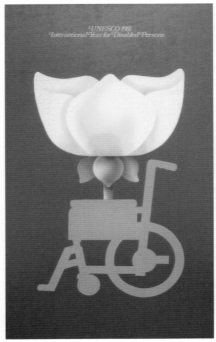

Designing a poster

Posters are like signs — both must give a clear message which can be read or interpreted at a reasonable distance. To do this, poster design should observe a few basic points. A successful poster must:

- attract attention
- be clear
- be simple

To attract attention, bright or contrasting colours should be used. There must also be a strong image or illustration.

Signpost

See Colour, page 16.

Poster lettering should be minimal and clear. Both the lettering and the image should reflect what the poster is about.

Signpost

See Lettering, page 202.

Posters usually carry some form of illustration. Posters without images are often boring, and defeat their whole purpose — to attract attention.

Integrated posters, using lettering and images, are probably the most successful.

Before designing a poster, it is important to know what its purpose is. A poster's purpose may be to seduce, to inform, to convince, to make an appeal, or to sell. Posters may be divided roughly into three main categories.

1. A general message poster (including propaganda)
2. A poster announcing an event
3. Pure advertising

General message posters

A general message poster usually gives a straight-forward message.

- Don't drink and drive.
- No smoking.
- Look after your health.
- AIDS information

Propaganda posters, such as those used during the two world wars, also give general messages.

Signpost

See 'The Pointing Posters', pages 220-221.

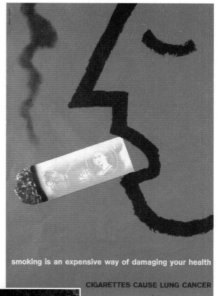

Do these anti-smoking posters get the message across?

Students' general message posters

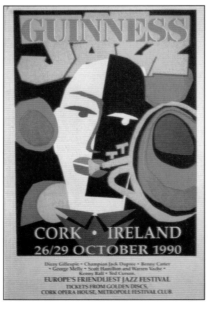

Event posters

An **event poster** is more specific than a general message poster. It is dealing with something that is going to happen at a certain time and place.

- a football match
- a disco or concert
- a fashion show
- a meeting

An event poster must contain the following information.

- What is it
- Where is it
- When is it (date)
- Time
- Admission charges (if any)
- Name of the organisation or group which is running or benefiting from the event — Amnesty International, the Lions Club.

A collage–type poster advertising an annual event in Ireland—The Guinness Cork Jazz Festival.

Pure advertising

Pure advertising posters relate to marketing a particular product or service.

- Erin Soups
- Solus Bulbs
- Butler's Irish Chocolates
- Credit Union
- Bord Failte

A professionally designed poster for Erin Soups.

Posters for the Credit Union designed by students.

A clear poster is a well-planned poster. The lettering must be easy to read. Avoid putting lettering in diagonal or vertical lines — these can be difficult to read.

Lettering (or each letter in one word) should be the same colour. Otherwise, the word will look disjointed and will not be easy to read.

For simplicity and legibility, cluttering should be avoided. The most successful posters are those which can be read at a glance and which are self-explanatory. The illustration should not consist of little bits of images scattered all over the place. A large illustration with well-placed lettering is much more successful.

Poster designers must get to know their audience. They should know whether their message is aimed at a certain age group, social class, special interest group or people with a particular level of income. For example, advertising for milk is usually aimed at the entire population, whereas Lego posters are aimed at children.

Suggested Assignment

Find examples of posters from each of the groups shown in this section. **Discuss** how they get their messages across.

Observe and Discuss

. . . the audiences at whom the posters you have collected are aimed. How do these posters get their messages across? Do they succeed or fail? Why?

Making a poster

Materials

You will need paper, a T square, a ruler, pencils and eraser.

For colour, you may use paint, markers, inks, pencils or collage, depending on your preference or the type of poster being designed.

Using a T square.

Ideas, layout and plans

Always jot down your ideas on paper first. Then start the initial planning on a small scale. Don't bother erasing your first attempts at putting your ideas down on paper. For one thing, it wastes time. But you may also find that some of the earlier ideas will be useful later.

When you are satisfied with your ideas, you should start doing the layout.

Illustrations should be worked into the poster as it is developing. They should not be added later as afterthoughts. It is easier to apply lettering *over* an illustration than vice-versa. Remember that most posters with lettering only can be a bit boring, unless the lettering is so creative that it becomes an illustration in itself.

Always use guidelines.

Remember to draw lightly when using guidelines. These must be erased later.

Lightly draw a margin of about 2 to 3cm all the way around the paper (depending on the size of your poster paper). If you do this first, you avoid the possibility of your lettering 'falling off' the edge of the paper (unless, of course, you want a particular effect!).

If your plan or layout includes centring words or illustrations, lightly draw a central line. It might be a good idea to do this anyway, as it will help you get the right balance.

Very few posters lack lettering. When working with letters, always use guidelines in the form of lines or complete grids.

The name of the general message, event or product is usually the most important lettering on the poster. Normally, this would be larger than any other lettering. It will also be in a more prominent position than any other lettering.

Signposts

See Painting, page 141.
See Composition, page 154.
See Lettering, page 192.

Avoid using too many lettering styles. Otherwise the poster may be too confusing.

Use bright, contrasting colours. Limiting the number of colours you use can be quite effective, producing a very sophisticated poster.

This poster was designed by a student who had received no tuition. Having studied poster design, what advice would you give this student?

Backgrounds for posters

If you decide not to work your illustration as a background to the lettering, you may wish to colour in the background with a wash. Geometric shapes also work well. Cut-outs or collage pieces can also be successful, especially as you can move these around before finally sticking them into place.

Signpost

See Painting, page 141.

As with all forms of design, you will need practice and time to experiment with the different techniques and materials.

Suggested Assignments

Design the following posters, based on your chosen theme. The size should be A3 or A2.

1. A poster incorporating lettering and an illustrated backdrop (multicoloured).
2. A poster without words (two colours, plus black and white).
3. A poster with lettering only, carried out in a creative way (multicoloured).
4. A 'pointing' poster saying something about your chosen theme.

Support Studies

Album covers through the years

With the popularity of cassettes and CDs, album covers are not as common as they once were. But they will never lose their place in the history of graphic design. All album covers are square, measuring 310mm x 310mm. CD covers are usually reduced album covers. They measure 120mm x 120mm.

Lettering plays an important part on many album covers. On others, it is primarily the image which matters.

Signposts

See Colour, page 16.
See Photography, page 242.
See Lettering, page 192.

Originally, most album covers had a large photograph of the singer or musician, combined with the name. This Elvis Presley cover was produced in 1957.

Psychedelic colours were typical of the colourful, flower power, hippy 1960s. People also had fun trying to identify all the characters on the Beatles' *Sgt. Pepper* album in 1967.

The 1970s brought in a more sophisticated style, as in *Aladin Sane* by David Bowie, 1973.

A Celtic influence was used on Thin Lizzy's *Johnny The Fox* .

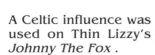

Elton John's *Captain Fantastic* (1975) incorporates the styles of Bosch and Surrealism. The lettering reminds us of a Beano comic.

Mike Oldfield's *Tubular Bells* uses hard-edge minimalism to produce a sophisticated effect.

A surrealistic interpretation of different aspects of Michael Jackson's world as seen through his own eyes. The *Dangerous* cover also includes selected pieces of other artists' work.

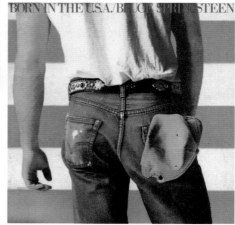

A revival of pride in the American way of life seems to be the message on Bruce Springsteen's *Born in the USA* (1984)— or is it?

230

Students' album cover designs

Suggested Assignments

1. Go to your local record store or look at your own collection of record covers. Put them into categories under the following headings.
   - portrait
   - logo
   - special image
   - all lettering
   - no lettering
   - a landscape or scene
   - other
2. Compare the different record or CD covers you have looked at and list their good and bad points. Give reasons why you think one cover is better than another.
3. Design an album or CD cover for one of the following.
   - gospel singers
   - heavy metal rock group
   - country and western singers
   - folk singers
   - rock group
   - group based on a special theme
4. Design a logo or a name (these could be the same, like 'Chicago') for a group.

Cassette and video covers both have formats which are rectangular. When you have designed your album or CD cover, you might like to move onto covers for videos or cassettes.

Signpost

See Format, pages 71, 106.

Observe and Discuss

. . . any album covers of your choice. What qualities of the covers appeal to you?

. . . the differences between album, CD, cassette and video covers.

Support Studies

Stamps

A selection of Irish and foreign stamps. Discuss the shape, subject matter, countries of origin, lettering. How many themes can you identify?

Adhesive postage stamps have been around since 1840. Their main function is to prove that payment for delivery has been made to the postal service. But stamps also act as miniature ambassadors for their countries of origin. They are like tiny posters depicting many different subjects — sport, architecture, industry, history, art, love, Christmas, flora and fauna, transport and crafts.

Stamps are classified as either definitive or commemorative. **Definitive stamps** are the everyday, ordinary stamps. **Commemorative stamps** are issued to mark certain events or to highlight special subjects.

An Post issued these commemorative stamps in 1992. Identify the themes.

Support Studies

Lettering on stamps

With the exception of stamps from Great Britain, all stamps show their country of origin clearly printed. Other optional writing may include the name or details of the person or event shown on the stamp.

Signpost

See Stamps, page 232.

Design your own stamps

Most Irish commemorative stamps measure only 4cm by 3cm (including the perforations). But most stamp designers work to a scale which is much larger than this. When the design is complete, it is reduced to the required size by the printer. However, the designer must always think in terms of the final size, since not all designs will reduce well. To see what a design might look like in its real size, a photocopier with reducing facilities would be a great help.

Suggested Assignments

1. Make a collection of as many stamps as you can, both Irish and foreign.
2. Find out what the worst recent definitive stamps show.

Support Studies

Samples of Irish stamps

Here are some samples of Irish commemorative stamps. While a few are in 'odd' sizes, An Post has generally standardised the size of its stamps in recent years.

A 1969 stamp showing stained glass by *Evie Hone*. It was Ireland's biggest stamp to date and was criticised for its awkwardness.

This Europa 1980 stamp depicting George Bernard Shaw was controversial because it used a caricature of the writer.

In 1981, this stamp was issued to commemorate the 50th anniversary of An Oige, the Irish Youth Hostel Association.

The winner of the 'Love' stamp competition in 1987 was a student at St Brigid's College, Callan, Co. Kilkenny.

A special stamp was issued in 1990, The European Year of Tourism.

Irish Waterways were highlighted in 1986.

Stamps show a wide range of styles. By studying them, one can learn alot about design techniques, layout and lettering. These tiny, colourful pieces of paper contain a wealth of knowledge, including art, design and other fields which can range from natural history to architecture.

Observe and Discuss

. . . the style of lettering and number design on the stamps, and the relationship between them.
. . . any ten stamps of your choice.

Suggested Assignment

Design an Irish stamp using your own choice of subject. The proportions must be 4cm x 3cm — so you may use similar, but larger, proportions such as 8 x 6, 20 x 15 etc. Remember to use **bold lettering** for ÉIRE. Use clear figures for the price. Draw in the perforations using a circular button or coin.

Be aware of the position of any lettering used in the stamp design. Lettering and design should blend so that they complement each other.

Signpost

See Lettering, page 192.

These 'Love' stamps were designed by students.

First Day Cover Designs

People all over the world enjoy collecting stamps. In addition to modern, rare or old stamps, they are interested in collecting **First Day Covers**. These are special envelopes which are designed to carry new stamps on their first day of issue. To commemorate this day, First Day Covers are given special **cancellation marks**.

The design brief

For the Irish 1988 'Love' stamps which celebrate Valentine's Day, the brief was simple — the stamp should incorporate a clown, a postbox and 'love'. The designs were treated in cartoon style. This reflected the fun associated with love stamps and Valentine's Day. The design chosen for the First Day Cover was also used for An Post's Philatelic Bulletin cover.

Like any other design project, several ideas were submitted before a final design was agreed.

The illustrations show: **top**—some design ideas; **middle**—work in progress on the final design; **bottom**—the First Day Cover, designed by Clodagh Holahan, was sent to thousands of people, both in Ireland and around the world.

Support Studies

Book jackets and covers

Like posters, album covers, and video covers, book jackets deal with words (lettering) and pictures (visuals). Unlike a poster, a book is viewed close up. This means that a book jacket or cover may carry a large amount of detail, if desired.

Most books are seen for the first time on shelves in a bookshop. Depending on how they are displayed, it may be the spine, and not the front, which is on view. When designing a book jacket, as much care must be taken with the spine as with the front.

Before beginning any design work, take a look at some book jackets, or **dust covers** as they are sometimes called. You will discover that a **book jacket** is broken up into five different parts.
- front • spine
- back • two flaps (front and back)

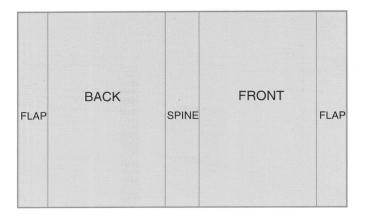

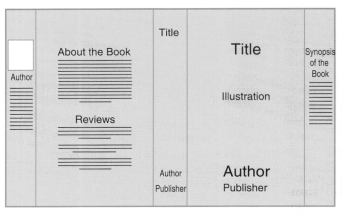

A **book cover** has only three parts — front, back and spine.

The title and author appear both on the front and on the spine. The publisher's name and/or logo may also appear on the front, but it always appears on the spine. Some extra information may also appear on the front — like 'Best seller' or 'The complete works'. The back usually contains a little more detail about the contents of the book, and perhaps the contents of reviews. Information about the author is usually found either on the back or on the back flap.

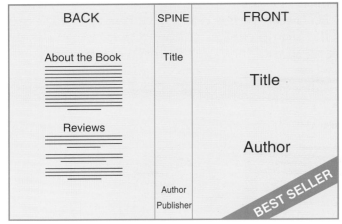

Once you are aware of what to put where on your book jacket, you must then think about the layout. What illustration or lettering should be used? What medium will be used (paint, pencils, ink, collage, photographs)? What style? There are so many choices to make! It might help you to look at some book jackets like those in the photograph and see if these will give you some inspiration.

Cut-outs or paste-ups are a good idea, as they will save you time.

Book jackets often tell a bit about the text. Sometimes they contain reviewers' comments. You could cut pieces of text out of a newspaper or magazine and put these in the place of the text.

Look at the lettering section. This will help you with your choice of typeface.

Layout, lettering, spacing, image and colour are all important in designing book covers or book jackets.

Signpost

See Lettering, page 192.

Illustration accommodating lettering.

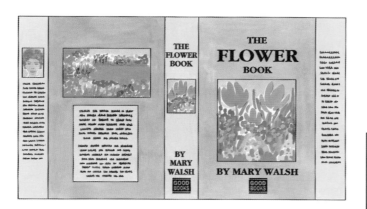

Lettering and illustration separate.

Lettering superimposed on illustration.

Suggested Assignments

1. Collect examples of book jackets or covers.
2. Design a book jacket on a theme of your choice. Use any of the techniques described in this book. You may want to think about inventing your own style or technique, as long as it contains all the necessary information.

Try using some form of printing when creating your book jacket.

Observe and Discuss

. . . the examples you have collected and designed.

Support Studies

Packaging

The primary purpose of packaging is to protect or contain the product. More and more, however, the secondary cosmetic purpose is gaining in importance, especially as a marketing ploy.

When planning a package, the designer must be able to visualise it as a 3D finished product. But he or she must also be able to see what it will look like in its flat, 2D form. It is this flat form which will eventually be printed and then folded into the final 3D shape.

Packaging involves graphic design in the form of lettering and/or images. As with all kinds of visual design, colour plays a vital role. It can serve to attract the attention of potential buyers. It can also be used to give desirable associations to the product — for example, blue and white with washing products (for cleanliness), or green with toilet products (for freshness and environmental friendliness), or red and yellow with hot food.

Suggested Assignments

1. Design a box to contain a shampoo bottle. Highlight environmental friendliness in the decoration.
2. Design a box which can be folded up to hold a cake which is 20cm in diameter. Highlight the baker's name or logo.
3. Design a package suitable for a light bulb. If one is available, use an old light bulb to get the correct dimensions. Use only two colours in your decoration.
4. Design an Easter egg box to hold an egg which is about 15cm high. Your decorations should keep children in mind. You may use unlimited colours.

Observe and Discuss

1. Visit your local supermarket or grocery shop. Observe and examine the packaging for a variety of items — soft drinks, soap powders, shampoos and toiletries, cereals, biscuits etc.
2. Open up a package — a cereal packet, for example. Find out what it looks like as a flattened, 2D shape.

Comment on the packaging shown in this picture.

Support Studies

Graphic Designers and Graphic Artists

Graphic designers, also known as commercial artists, are design specialists. It is their job to impart visual information to a large number of people. The main function of their designs is a commercial one.

Artists sometimes use graphics as a means of self-expression. They create works of art which are printed in limited quantities, using techniques such as etching, screen printing or lithography.

Signposts

See Printing, page 172.
See Rembrandt etching, page 175.
See M. C. Escher, pages 132, 140, 161.

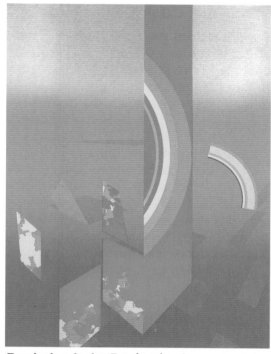

Borderlands, by Benjamin. Screen print. CCA Galleries, London.

artist's name   date   number of print - this one is the 10th in a series of 15

All prints should contain this information.

Dorset Cove, John Brunsdon. Lithograph. CCA Galleries, London.

The graphic artist usually takes the process from beginning to end. Because the prints are made by hand, they may vary slightly. Each print is then signed, dated and numbered by the artist.

239

Industrial design and product design

The **industrial designer** works in industry. He or she designs everything from bathroom fittings to bicycles, from hi-fi equipment to hair dryers, from fuel containers to furniture.

The first concern of the industrial designer is the function of the item being designed. 'Form follows function' — so the design of any item should reflect its function.

In the past, craftspeople designed their products and saw the whole process — from design to finished product — through to completion. Today, however, the design of so many items such as cars or aeroplanes has become very complex. Industrial designers now find themselves as part of a team with specialists such as engineers, mechanics and physicists.

The history of transport provides us with a good example of how the development of a product is linked to its function. Sometimes, the functions may change, leading to new design concepts. New materials may also provide opportunities for designers to give their talents more scope.

Suggested Assignment

Trace the development of the telephone. Remember that 'Form follows function'.

Observe and Discuss

1. Is there any item you use frequently which you feel is particularly well-designed *or* badly designed?
2. Look at the recent developments in the design of hi-fi equipment.
3. Is there any product on the market today which you think could become a design classic in the future?

Design Classics

Some products are called **design classics**. Their shapes or forms have stood the test of time. Years after these designs were created, they are still recognisable.

The Barcelona chair.

The Volkswagen 'beetle'.

The Coca-Cola bottle.

Levi 501 jeans.

Support Studies

Fashion design

Fashion designers work in the clothing industry. Fashions in clothing change quite often, so these people must always create new designs.

The fashion industry is a product of our wealthy Western society. The primary function of clothing, of course, is to protect our bodies from the elements. But today, the secondary function of clothing — as decoration — has taken over.

Fashion designers deal with many different types of clothing — formal wear, casual wear, daywear and evening wear, sportswear and rainwear. They work with many different fabrics. They have to consider the use to which a garment will be put. They must think about colour, cut and fabric, as well as price, durability and washability.

Some fashion designers specialise in accessories — things like shoes, bags, hats and jewellery.

Jewellery is often much more than just an accessory to fashion. The top jewellery designers are actually sculptors who work with precious metal and stones.

Observe and Discuss

. . . the markets at which these fashion photographs are aimed. Are any particular fashion items being highlighted?

Photography

Louise Brooks, E. R. Ritchee. The Kobal Collection.

Support Studies

The history of photography

We are surrounded by visual imagery — this book is just one example. These images would not exist without **photography** — a word which means 'drawing with light'.

The **camera obscura** (dark chamber) became popular as an aid to sketching in the eighteenth century. This was a box with a lens at one end and a sheet of paper at the other. The camera obscura was pointed at the scene and the outline of the scene was drawn onto the paper.

In this old print, an entire room has been converted into a camera obscura which is being used as an aid to sketching.

In 1750, the Italian artist Canaletto (1697–1768) used the camera obscura to help him achieve a better perspective in his paintings of Venice. The idea of the camera dates back even further. In 1515, Leonardo da Vinci described the camera obscura. Even earlier, in 400 BC, a pinhole was used instead of a lens.

In the early 1750s, it was discovered that the chemical, silver nitrate, was light sensitive. In 1790, Thomas Wedgwood made **photograms** by placing objects on white leather which had been sensitised with silver nitrate.

In 1826, a French doctor, Nicéphore Niepce (1765–1833), produced the world's first photograph using a camera obscura and an eight-hour exposure.

Niepce's first camera.

Niepce's earliest surviving photograph, dated 1826, shows the view from his window.

L.J.M. Daguerre (1787–1851) was a French pioneer of photography. He produced the first **daguerreotype** camera photographs in 1838. A daguerreotype is a photograph in which the impression is taken on a silver plate which has been sensitised with iodine and developed by vapour of mercury.

The **daguerreotype** is a one-off photographic image. Daguerre went on to form a partnership with Niepce in 1829.

A daguerreotype picture of Daguerre himself, taken in 1848.

William Henry Fox Talbot (1800–1877) was the father of modern photography. He used salt and silver nitrate to sensitise paper. Fox Talbot invented the first negative/positive method of photography called the **calotype**. It used a wax paper negative and a paper-based photograph. This was the first multi-copy method of photography. It was patented in 1841.

This image of leaves was the first reproduced photograph.

Fox Talbot had made **photograms** several years before Daguerre. A photogram is a picture on photographic material created by means of exposing it to light but without using a camera. This produced a negative print. This in turn was **contact printed** to produce a positive image.

The Fox Talbot studio at Reading, England, around 1845.

In 1842, Fox Talbot set up a photographic studio. He took pictures of buildings by putting paper into a camera obscura. He kept reducing the exposure time until there was no visible image evident on the paper. Then, one day, Fox Talbot went to resensitise a piece of paper that had already been exposed to light. Lo and behold, a picture started to emerge. Fox Talbot had discovered how to develop a photograph.

Signposts

See The photographic process, pages 248- 49.
See Contact printing, page 252.

The Pencil of Nature by Fox Talbot was the first book of photographs. It was published in 1844. Fox Talbot also made instantaneous photographs in 1851 and photo engravings in 1852.

In 1851, Fredrick Scott Archer, an English sculptor, announced his new **wet collodion photographic process**. Although his process was not patented, it replaced both the calotype and the daguerreotype. It reduced exposure time from minutes to seconds and tenths of seconds.

Early war photography

Mathew Brady (1823–1896) was an American pioneer of photography. He used a wagon to carry his photographic equipment to the battlefields of the American Civil War in the 1860s. Brady worked with wet plates. So he had to transport the chemicals for preparing and developing the plates with him at all times.

Manning the cannon at Yorktown, May 1862.

In 1861, Brady photographed these Yankee soldiers and their families at a camp in Pennsylvania.

The horror of war—a dead rebel sharpshooter photographed by Brady at Gettysburg in July 1863.

These three rebel soldiers survived the Battle of Gettysburg.

The original No.1 Kodak camera, shown here with a roll of film, was perfected in 1888 and went on sale in 1889.

Support Studies

Other important dates in photography

1877　The first piece of photojournalism was published. It was entitled 'Street Life in London'.

1889　The Kodak No. 1 camera and roll film was produced in the US by the Eastman Company. This was the first hand-held camera. It became popular with ordinary people very quickly.

1924　The German Leica, a 35mm camera, was launched. It was small, dependable, and had a range of different lenses.

1935　The electronic flash was invented in the US, as was Kodachrome colour transparency film.
　　　Social documentary photographs of the plight of poor tenant farmers in the midwest of America were taken.

California, 1936 by Dorothea Lange. Lange photographed the desperate plight of poor migrant workers during America's Great Depression.

Like Dorothea Lange, Arthur Rothstein also took pictures for the Farm Security Administration. This 1936 photograph is entitled *Farmer and sons walking in dust storm, Cimarron, Oklahoma.*

1947 The black and white instant Polaroid process was invented.

1955 Kodak Tri-X black and white film with a speed of 200ASA was invented.

1959 The zoom lens was invented.

1960 Polaroid introduced a 60-second self-processing colour film.
The laser was invented in the US, making holography possible.

1985 Minolta introduced the first body-integrated autofocus single lens reflex (SLR) camera in Japan.

New cameras and lenses have made underwater photography possible. This is a 'Big Eye' resting on a Stag's Head Coral.

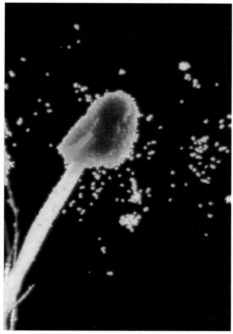

Time-lapse photography—pollen being dispersed from a willow stamen.

A pheasant's feather magnified 15 times.

The flower of the fleabane as humans see it; and photographed in ultra-violet light. Bees see mainly yellow and blue, plus ultra-violet.

The photographic process

Making photographs is both simple and exciting. Photographs can be made using photographic paper, light and chemicals. The light-sensitive paper is exposed to light, then developed in the chemicals.

The photographer's basic equipment. Discuss what is shown here.

What you will need

1. Photographic paper — ordinary paper coated with light-sensitive emulsion. (Never take this out of its package until you are ready to use it. The light will ruin it.)
2. Developer
3. Fixer
4. Measuring jug
5. Water
6. 3 deep trays. Each tray should be large enough to hold a sheet of photographic paper and enough solution to completely cover the paper.
7. 2 plastic tongs — these are used to transfer the paper from one tray to another.
8. A reasonably dark room — total darkness is obviously the best.

Organising your work area

1. Line the working area with old newspapers.
2. Clearly label all three trays.
   1 Developer   2 Water   3 Fixer
3. Label the tongs. One pair is for use in the *developing tray only*. The other pair is for the rinse and fix trays. *The fixer must not come into contact with the developer.* Even as little as a few drops will ruin the developer.
4. Mix developer and fixer following the manufacturer's instructions. Do not carry trays of solution about. Don't splash.
5. Always use tongs and not fingers.
6. Wash hands after using chemicals.

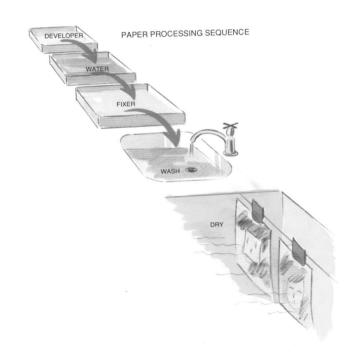

Photographic paper

Photographic paper is light-sensitive. It will darken if exposed to light. When purchased, photographic paper is packed inside a black plastic bag. Each sheet of paper must be taken from the bag in darkness or when using a **safety light**.

A small amount of light will make an image on the paper, although this cannot be seen. When the paper is put into the developer, the image is strengthened so that it can be seen.

Developing an image on paper

During developing, the print should be moved about in the solution using the correct tongs. The paper should stay in the developer until there is either a high contrast of black and white, or the desired tone, depending on the grade of paper (0 = soft, 5 = hard).

After developing, a quick rinse in water will remove most of the developer. Here we are using water instead of a stop bath.

Then the paper is put into the fixer. This stops the paper from being light-sensitive. It also makes the image permanent.

Finally, wash the paper for a few minutes. Then let it dry at room temperature.

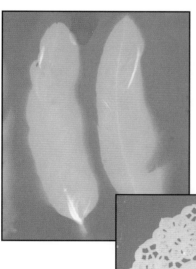

Sun pictures made by students. Do you recognise the objects they used?

Sun pictures

Sun pictures are made by covering parts of the photographic paper with an object and exposing the rest of the paper to sunlight.

Suitable objects for sun pictures are flowers, leaves, grasses, cut-paper stencils, keys, lace etc.

Developer is not needed for this experiment. To make the image permanent, place the paper in a tray of fixer for a few minutes. Then rise in clean water.

Materials

photographic paper
black changing bag (or black plastic sack)
suitable objects — flowers, leaves etc.
piece of board
piece of glass or perspex
tray of fixer
tongs for handling paper
water

Method

1. Mix tray of fixer with enough volume to cover the paper.
2. Work out the layout of your shapes on ordinary paper.
3. Take out a sheet of photographic paper, using a changing bag in a darkened room.
4. Put photographic paper onto board, emulsion side up.
5. Transfer your shapes onto the photographic paper.
6. Cover with glass or perspex to keep shapes in position.
7. Place in the sunshine or bright daylight.
8. Leave exposed until the paper has turned a dark colour. This could take anything from half a minute to half an hour.
9. When the background is dark, take off your shapes and place the paper in the tray of fixer.
10. Leave to fix for a few minutes (following manufacturer's instructions).
11. Wash thoroughly in clean water.

Chemograms

Chemograms are the pictures produced when objects are soaked in either developer or fixer and then placed on photographic paper in a darkened room.

Developer speeds up the darkening process caused by light on photographic paper. **Fixer** stops the photographic paper from being sensitive to light or developer. Fixer is used to make the photographic image permanent. If fixer is applied to any part of the photographic paper before the developer, then that part of the paper will not darken.

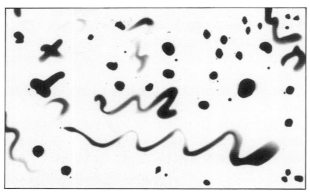

These chemogram images were made by using developer on photographic paper.

Developer on paper

Materials

photographic paper
black changing bag (or black plastic sack)
paint brushes, leaves, any variety of objects
small container of developer
tray of fixer
tray of water
tongs

Method

1. Take out a sheet of photographic paper using the changing bag in a darkened room.
2. Make experiments on the paper by using one of these methods.
   (a) Make a pattern of dots on the paper by splashing developer on it.
   (b) Draw directly onto the paper, using a brush dipped in developer.
   (c) Dip leaves and objects into developer and press against the paper.
3. When the marks on the paper have darkened fully, rinse the paper in a tray of water.
4. Transfer the paper to the tray of fixer for a few minutes to make the image permanent.
5. Wash thoroughly in clean water and hang to dry.

This chemogram was made by dipping a leaf in fixer and then placing it on photographic paper.

Fixer on paper

Materials

photographic paper
black changing bag (or black plastic sack)
brushes, leaves, variety of shapes and objects
small container of fixer
tray of developer
tray of water
tray of fixer
two sets of tongs

Method

1. Take out a sheet of photographic paper using the changing bag in a darkened room.
2. Make experiments on paper using these methods.
   (a) Draw a picture on the paper using a paint brush dipped in fixer.
   (b) Dip objects — leaves etc. — in the fixer and place on the paper.
3. Wait for one/two minutes. Then thoroughly wash the paper in water. As this paper is about to be processed, it is very important to make sure that no fixer comes in contact with the developer. As little as a few drops of fixer are enough to ruin a full tray of developer.
4. Process the paper in the normal way — developer, rinse, fix, wash.

Photograms

Photograms are sometimes called **shadow pictures**. They are made by covering parts of the photographic paper with objects and exposing the remainder of the paper to artificial light. The paper is then processed in the usual way — developer, rinse, fix, wash.

The most suitable objects for photograms are keys, coins etc., as they are completely **opaque**. With opaque objects, the paper under them will stay completely white, regardless of the amount of exposure time or the development time given to the paper.

Photograms are similar to sun pictures. But instead of the long exposure time needed in sun pictures, the paper is exposed for just a few seconds. Developer is then used to strengthen the image.

Translucent objects such as leaves will reduce the amount of light reaching the paper. (A translucent object will let light pass through it, but it is not transparent.) When a photogram of a translucent object is developed, the background will be completely black, while the area under the object will be a shade of grey. If translucent objects are overexposed, the area under them will turn black when developed.

Materials

photographic paper
black changing bag (or black plastic sack)
suitable opaque or translucent objects
piece of board
piece of glass or perspex
desk lamp with 40 watt bulb
tray of developer
tray of water
tray of fixer
two sets of tongs

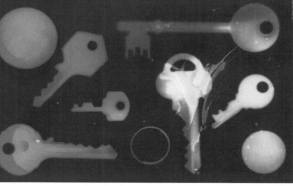

Samples of students' photograms.

Method

1. In a darkened room, take out a sheet of photographic paper using the changing bag. Place on the board, emulsion side up.
2. Place objects on the paper. Leaves may need a sheet of glass placed over them to keep them in contact with the paper.
3. Expose to light for two seconds from a distance of about 40cm. A longer time can be used with a lower watt bulb placed farther away. The sharpest results are achieved using a small light source at a greater distance from the paper.
4. Process the paper in the normal way — developer, rinse, fix, wash.

Contact printing

A **photogram** gives you a negative image. To reverse the black and white areas, a **contact print** may be made.

Materials

A safety light — You can make a safety light by covering a 15 watt bulb with a sheet of red transparent material. *The safety light should always be kept at least a metre away from any photographic paper.*

photograms
sheet of glass
tray of developer
tray of fixer
tray of water
2 sets of tongs

Method

1. Using a safety light, place a sheet of photographic paper on a table.
2. Place the photogram face down on the photographic paper.
3. Use a sheet of glass to keep the photogram in contact with the paper. This will help to get a sharp image.
4. Expose the paper with the light vertically above it.
5. Process paper — developer, rinse, fix, wash.

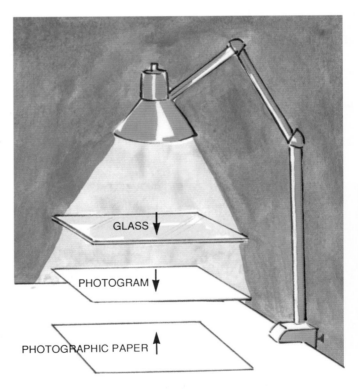

GLASS ↓

PHOTOGRAM ↓

PHOTOGRAPHIC PAPER ↑

Reflection printing uses a magazine page instead of a photogram. The magazine page/picture is placed on the bottom, as it has print on the back of it. The photographic paper is placed above it, emulsion side facing downwards.

Pinhole camera

So far we have experimented with photographic paper, light and chemicals. We will now make a **pinhole camera**. This is the first step towards taking a conventional picture.

A pinhole camera is a black box with a small pinhole at one end. The photographic paper is placed at the opposite end of the box.

The image is formed by light passing through the pinhole onto the paper.

The photographic paper should be marked at one end. This will show that the image is created upside down on the paper.

The distance from the pinhole to the back of the box determines how much of the scene can be recorded.

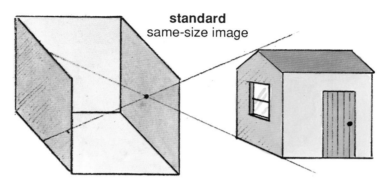

standard
same-size image

If the distance between the pinhole and the paper is equal to the distance between the pinhole and the object, then the image will be the same size.

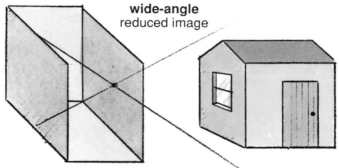

wide-angle
reduced image

If the object is farther away from the pinhole than the paper - for example, a house - then the picture will be of a wide-angle, reduced image.

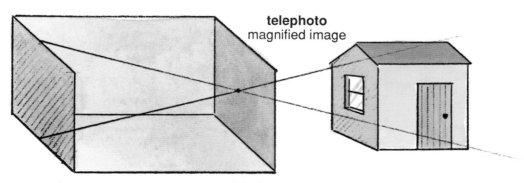

telephoto
magnified image

If the image is closer to the pinhole than the paper is, then the image will be magnified.

Making a pinhole camera

Materials

a box with a deep-fitting lid (a shoebox would
be ideal)

black paint with a matt finish

paint brush

flat, thin piece of metal that can be cut with a
scissors (a mineral can or similar)

compass point or needle

black tape

emery paper

Blu-tack

scissors

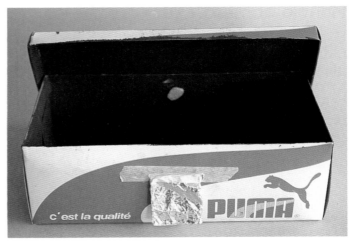

A pinhole camera made by a student.

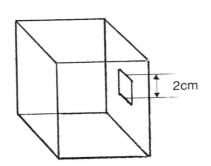

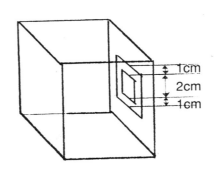

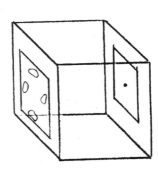

Method

1. Cut out a hole about 2cm² from the front of the box.
2. Cut out a 4cm² piece of metal. Prick the metal in the centre with the compass point or needle. The size of the pinhole affects the quality of the picture. It is better to err on the side of too small rather than too large.
3. Smooth both sides of the metal with emery paper.
4. Tape the metal sheet over the hole on the inside of the box.
5. Paint the inside of the box and the lid with black paint. Allow to dry. Unblock the pinhole, if necessary.
6. On the outside of the box, tape a shutter across the pinhole with black tape.
7. Attach a sheet of photographic paper to the back of the box, opposite the pinhole, using Blu-tack. The emulsion side should face the pinhole. Remember to work in safety light when removing and attaching photographic paper.
8. Fit lid securely.

The camera is now ready to take a photograph.

Taking a picture with a pinhole camera

Choose a fairly bright day. Decide on the subject of your picture. Place the camera on a firm surface facing the subject. *The camera must be kept absolutely still during the exposure.* A brick or any flat object similar in weight should be placed on the lid to keep it still.

When the camera is in place, lift the tape shutter. This allows the paper to be exposed to light. The length of time you expose the picture is all a matter of experimentation. A number of things affect the finished picture — the size of the pinhole, the sensitivity of the paper, the brightness of the day and the distance between the pinhole and the paper.

You could start your exposure experiment as shown in the chart below.

When the exposure time is up, cover the pinhole with the tape shutter.

Day	Minutes
very bright	2
bright	3
dull	4
very dull	6

Processing

In the safety light, remove the paper from the pinhole camera. Process it in the normal way — developer, rinse, fix, wash.

The picture you get will be a **negative** of the subject taken. To get a **positive** image, make a contact print.

Signpost

See Contact printing, page 252.

Common faults

Pinhole cameras aren't always fool-proof. You may discover that you have had a problem or two. The chart shows a few of the problems, plus the solutions.

Problem	Possible cause	Solution
black all over	stray light	Check fit of camera lid.
too light	not enough exposure	Lengthen exposure time.
too dark	too much exposure	Shorten exposure time.
blurred	camera or object moved during exposure	Secure camera; choose stationary object.
streaks of black	light leaking into camera	Hold camera up to the light and check for punctured surface area.

What about lens sizes?

Photographers can choose from a wide variety of cameras and lens sizes today. Many cameras allow the photographer to use different lenses. The type of image will depend on the type of lens.

. . . how different lens sizes give different pictures.

The only way to photograph a leopard — with a long lens!

A Joshua tree photographed with a fish-eye lens.

The same location—Hickman Bridge, Utah— photographed with (left) a wide-angle lens and (right) a standard lens.

A dragonfly captured close-up with a macro lens.

Suggested Assignment

Collect as many brochures as you can from camera shops. Discuss the many different types of cameras and lenses on the market. Which one would suit you —or your class?

256

Three-dimensional (3D) Work

Comfort (1986), Clodagh Holahan. Bronze on limestone, 16cm.

Support Studies

Photographs and paintings are flat. They have two dimensions — length and breadth. Some works have another dimension — depth. These works are called **three-dimensional**. The most obvious examples of three-dimensional work are pieces of sculpture and architecture.

A síle-na-gig from Cashel, Co. Tipperary. Little is known about these carvings, although some suggest they may be fertility symbols.

The Discus Thrower, Greek, 5th century BC. The Greeks always looked for perfection in the human form.

Tribute to W.B. Yeats, Henry Moore (1898 - 1986). St Stephen's Green, Dublin.

A sculpture outside the museum in Cleveland, Ohio.

What is 3D?

- 3D = length by breadth by depth.
- 3D takes up space, while 2D work is flat.
- 3D work has its own depth, while 2D work may give an *illusion* of depth.

 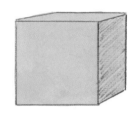

Support Studies

Other examples of three-dimensional work

When we think of three-dimensional work, we often confine ourselves to sculpture. But there are many other art forms which are also three-dimensional.

These puppets were designed by Alice Power.

Everyday objects like these are three-dimensional.

Support Studies

Three-dimensional work may be functional, decorative, or both. It covers many things, including puppetry, stage sets and jewellery. All areas such as these have an **aesthetic quality** (a sense of beauty), but they also need to be functional in a decorative and artistic way.

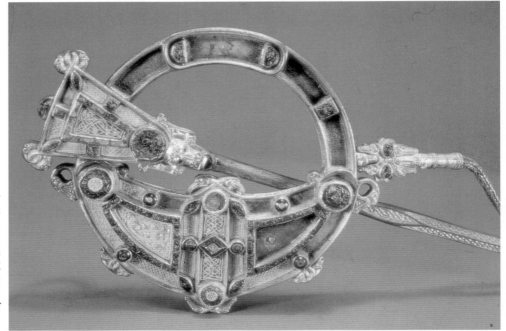

The Tara Brooch, a three-dimensional piece with a wonderful aesthetic quality. Dating from the 8th century, it consists of a ring and a long, straight pin. It was cast in silver with gold panels and glass studs. It can be seen in the National Museum of Ireland.

This children's playground was designed by landscape architect Sally Visick.

Suggested Assignments

1. Collect pictorial examples of 3D items from magazines and newspapers.

2. Pottery, metalwork and woodwork have practical uses in our homes. Collect pictures of these 3D examples from magazines or newspapers.

Support Studies

Relief Work

Relief work is also a form of 3D. Relief work is attached to a 2D background or surface. Relief work is often described as a half-way point between 2D and 3D.

There are three kinds of relief work.

- **Intaglio** — This is when the 'sculpture' is actually sunken into the background.

- **High relief** — This stands out a greater distance from its background. While it is attached to its background, it has developed an almost independent existence.

Part of *The Well of Moses*, Klaus Sluter (d. 1406). This sculpture is almost free-standing. Sluter gave his work bulk and volume. His drapery and facial expressions are lifelike.

Nefertiti: adoring the sun (14th century BC) is a good example of intaglio. Note how the images are chiselled into the limestone. Egyptian Museum, Cairo.

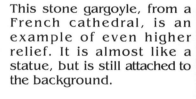

This stone gargoyle, from a French cathedral, is an example of even higher relief. It is almost like a statue, but is still attached to the background.

- **Low relief** — The sculpture is slightly raised against a background.

The Creation, Lorenzo Ghiberti (1378-1455). This gilt bronze high relief is just one panel from *The Gates of Paradise* series on the doors of the Baptistry, Florence.

Other examples of relief

Coins and medals } low relief
Cameo brooches }
Plaques and fireplace panels } medium or high relief

Support Studies

From relief to 3D

During the Renaissance, sculpture began to free itself from the confines of structures such as architecture. It was often found in **niches** in churches or grand houses where it was meant to be viewed from one side only.

St George, Donatello (c.1386–1466). This figure was carved for The Florentine Guild of Armourers. It stands in a niche in the Church of San Michele. The relaxed, casual pose shocked people at the time.

David, Donatello (c. 1386–1466). Bronze, 160cm (5.25ft). Bargello, Florence. Donatello's David looks more like the young boy who slew Goliath.

David, Michelangelo (1475–1564). Marble, 411cm (13.5ft). Accademia, Florence. Michelangelo shows David standing proud, after the Greek tradition.

Sculpture in the round — free-standing sculpture

Sculpture finally became an independent, free-standing work of art, as it had once been during classical times.

Observe and Discuss

. . . the difference between relief and free-standing sculpture.
. . . the two Davids.
. . . the differences between the two sculptures by Donatello.

Support Studies

Examples of Irish High Crosses

These crosses show examples of intaglio and low relief work on free-standing 3D forms.

Carndonagh High Cross — 6th century: This sandstone cross looks as if it has just broken away from a block of stone. It is a simple cross, showing an intricate ribbon design on top. The whole surface is covered with some form of decoration. The figures near the base are simple and not very realistic.

Ahenny High Cross — 8th century: Apart from the base, the whole surface of the Ahenny High Cross (sandstone) is covered with different decorative patterns. It has a wheel at the intersection and an unusual capstone. Fine studs show an influence from metalwork technique.

Moone High Cross — 9th century: This is a very tall, slim cross made of granite with a small wheel at the intersection. It is thought that the 51 panels were used to tell/show illiterate people stories from the Bible. Both animals and people are depicted in an abstract way. The panel with the 12 apostles at the base is full of rhythm and pattern. It is a wonderful use of space.

Monasterboice High Cross —10th century: This quartz-sandstone cross is a broad wheel cross, divided into panels. The decoration is figurative. The figures are carved deeply into the stone, giving a high relief effect. The scenes on the cross are from the Old and New Testaments.

Relief work is still used to decorate architecture.

Suggested Assignments

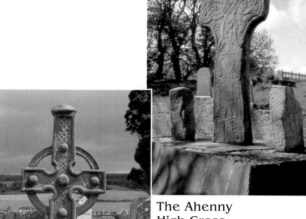

The Carndonagh High Cross, Co. Donegal.

The Ahenny High Cross, Co. Tipperary.

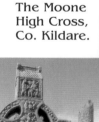

The Moone High Cross, Co. Kildare.

St Muirdeach's Cross, Monasterboice, Co. Louth.

1. Collect pictorial examples of relief sculpture.
2. Find a piece of relief work which is suitable for rubbing. Take a rubbing from it.

Signposts

See Rubbings, page 87.
See Texture, page 80.

Support Studies

Three-dimensional work in Art, Craft, Design covers the following processes:
- additive
- subtractive
- constructional

Additive — The additive process involves building up a form or shape with modelling materials such as clay, plasticine, papier mâché, plaster of Paris or wax.

Subtractive — This process involves carving or taking away material to make a form or shape. Suitable materials for subtractive work include soap, plaster block, polystyrene, wood, stone and wax.

Subtractive sculpture: very little is known about the massive statues on Easter Island. They were carved from grey volcanic stone. Some are 9m (30ft) tall.

Constructional — Constructional work is the most versatile of 3D work. Almost any material can be used — paper, cardboard, sponge, various types of wire, metal, wood. Many joining materials may be used to attach the pieces together. These include: glues, staples, pins, nails, wire, bolts, rivets, thread and string.

Sculptures in bronze by F.E. McWilliam, *Women of Belfast*. Additive gesture sculpture — frozen in time.

In *Women of Belfast,* a series of bronze pieces by F.E. McWilliam, a bomb explodes in a room full of women. Just look at what happened. It is as if we are experiencing a few split seconds in time — then waiting in vain for the bodies to come to rest — which, of course, they will never do.

Bronze isn't usually associated with such energy. Because it is a heavy metal, we tend to associate it with more solid, weighty works.

Observe and Discuss

. . . your reactions to *Women of Belfast.*

Support Studies

Additive work

Modelling

When creating a **model** (a built-up, 3D piece of work) we must first consider the materials we are using.

Examples of modelling materials
- **Clay** — suitable for large or small-scale work, broad or fine detail.
- **Plasticine** — suitable for small-scale work only because of the quantities needed.
- **Papier mâché** — suitable for large-scale, light-weight work — puppets, masks etc. Can be used on its own or on a wire base.

- **Plaster** — suitable for small or large-scale work. Can be used wet for free modelling or for casting a piece of work in clay (to give it permanency).

Signpost

See Casting, page 267.

- **Gypsona** (plaster bandage) — suitable for large or small works. Can be used on its own, or on/over a base or structure, or draped over a wire construction.
- **Wax** — suitable for large or small pieces. Very difficult to control, as it has to be used in a melted or pliable form. Would need to be worked quickly.

Clay

Natural clays vary quite a bit. Some natural clays tend to fall apart or dry too quickly. Unless one works fast, such clay is not suitable for modelling. **Grog clay** or **stoneware clay**, which is usually grey, will put up with a lot more handling than most other clays. All clays should be **wedged** or **kneaded** before use. This eliminates air bubbles and makes the clay more workable.

Signpost

See Pottery, page 320.

Today, synthetic clay is produced especially for modelling. It contains small pieces of fibre which hold the clay together. When left to dry, it doesn't crack or split like natural clays.

Regardless of what kind of clay you decide to use, all clays must be kept air-tight after each working session. Do this by covering the clay with a sheet of plastic, a damp cloth, or both. Natural clay should be dried gradually. Otherwise, it may dry unevenly and parts of it may fall off. At no time should a piece of wet clay be added to a dry piece, as it will not stick.

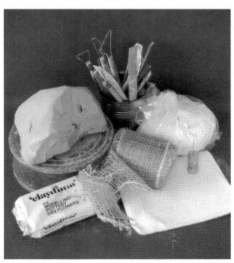

Some of the materials needed for modelling clay.

Modelling with clay

It is surprising how simple it is to model something in clay. Though it falls into the 'additive' category, there are also times when clay has to be taken away — as when too much has been put in a place where it is not needed. The easiest way to add clay is in pieces which are rolled out in 'worm-like' shapes.

If a piece of modelling has protruding pieces, it will need support. Supports vary, depending on the structure of the piece. Supports are known as **armatures**.

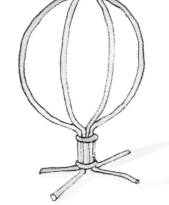

An armature like this will support anything head-shaped. Useful for masks.

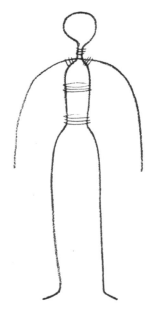

An armature made of wire can be used for figure modelling.

When starting to model in clay, why not start with a piece of clay about the size of your fist? Form a small, simple animal from this, such as a mouse, cat or hedgehog.

A hedgehog is a good starting point for modelling in clay.

A first-year student made this imaginative funny face with modelling clay.

Support Studies

Natural clay can be fired at a very high temperature and made into a hard substance. Once it has been fired, it can never revert to its 'clay' state again.

When firing a clay model, it is a good idea to make your piece hollow, keeping an even thickness of clay and avoiding air bubbles.

Clay may be worked with the hands and fingers. If you want a certain smooth finish or textured surface, you will need a few basic tools. The tools used in clay modelling are similar to those used in pottery.

Signpost

See Pottery tools, page 325.

Casting

All clay models can be cast. A **cast** involves making a plaster model of the clay object by first making a negative mould of the object. This in turn is filled with plaster to make a positive image or form. The simpler the form, the easier it will be to cast. Otherwise you may end up with a jig-saw of moulds which would prove difficult to work, even for the most experienced craftsperson.

Signpost

See Modelling with plaster, page 269.

Suggested Assignment

With the aid of a wire frame (armature), make a figure of a person digging.

Standing figure with basket, a student's work.

Head with hair 'flying', made by a student.

Support Studies

A student made this head from a multi-coloured piece of plasticine. The Theme is 'Fear'.

Plasticine

Most children have used plasticine to make models. It is similar to clay, although it is not as pliable. Its plasticity can be improved by gentle heating or by working well with the hands.

Plasticine is rarely used by artists, since it is seen as non-permanent. It can still be used to cast from, however.

Plasticine has one advantage over clay — it is much easier to recycle it and use it again. It is usually used for small pieces, as it is expensive for larger models.

Plasticine has been used very successfully in animated TV programmes. As the shapes can be easily changed (it does not dry out like clay), plasticine is very popular.

Today, a derivative of plasticine called FIMO is popular with students. It can be used to make jewellery and can be made permanent by firing at very low temperatures in a domestic oven.

A statue made of FIMO was part of one student's chosen theme. What might this theme be?

Suggested Assignment

Using plasticine, make an insect, a snail, a frog or some other life form which you might find in your garden.

Support Studies

Papier mâché

There are a few different approaches to modelling with **papier mâché** (in French, this means 'chewed paper').

The best known one is to mix torn strips of newspaper with ordinary wallpaper paste. (Follow manufacturer's instructions when mixing paste.) The strips of newspaper covered in the paste can then be hung over a wire frame, balloon or old light bulb (for puppets) to make a 3D shape which will dry hard.

Another way to make papier mâché is to pulp up the newspaper with paste (either wallpaper paste or wood glue) and turn it into a pliable material. This is then shaped and made into a form with the fingers.

An animal made by a student from papier mâché.

Different papers, like magazine paper or tissue paper, together with different pastes (like polybond or wood glue), can give different effects. By experimenting, you will discover what suits you best.

Fine mesh

Fine mesh wire (sometimes known as chicken wire or lettuce wire) is one of the best materials to use as a frame for papier mâché. It is good for small pieces, as well as for paper mâché sculptures over 30cm in any direction.

You will need a good pliers and a good wire cutters to work with the wire.

Suggested Assignments

1. Make a puppet's head out of paper mâché. Base your head on one of these characters: a witch, a chef, a sailor, a school teacher, a judge.
2. Class project: Make a large head — a dragon, perhaps — for a local festival or a school play . . . or just for fun.

Since papier mâché is light and easy to carry, it is often used to make carnival heads and dragons. These are made by placing pasted strips of newspaper over a fine-mesh wire frame for support.

Support Studies

Modelling with plaster

It is difficult to use plaster on its own for modelling because it sets so quickly. Some kind of support is usually needed to hold the plaster. This support frame, or armature, can then be covered with plaster, which will in turn be used to build up the required form.

Signpost

See armatures, page 266.

Plaster is more controllable when combined with a light-weight loose-weave cloth such as scrim. The scrim is dipped into the liquid plaster mixture, and is nearly ready for setting. It is then pulled across the frame (clay, cardboard, wire etc.).

There is a modern type of plaster of Paris called **gypsona** which is used by doctors to make plaster casts for broken limbs. This material consists of gauze, a type of bandage which has already been impregnated with plaster. The gauze can be cut into appropriate shapes while dry. Gypsona can be purchased at any chemist's shop. When one wishes to use it, all that one has to do is wet the gauze and arrange the strips as required on some kind of frame or armature. This way of working with gypsona lends itself to puppet-making.

Mixing plaster

Plaster : Water
50 : 50

When a mound or hill of plaster appears above the water surface, as shown in the diagram, it indicates that the ratio of water-to-plaster is in the correct proportion.

1. Add the plaster to the water by filtering the plaster through your fingers as you let it fall into the water. This lets the plaster dissolve gradually without becoming lumpy.
2. When the mound of plaster appears, leave the mixture to stand for a short while (max. 10 minutes).
3. Stir the mixture.
4. Check that it is properly mixed and that there are no lumps by placing your hand in it. If the plaster leaves a creamy, opaque coating on your hand, it should be ready for pouring — or for doing whatever you wish with it.

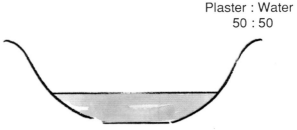

water level (before plaster is added)

displaced water level (after plaster is added)

Suggested Assignments

1. Pour plaster over a balloon, shaping it as it flows. Try to make it into a face shape.
2. Make a reclining figure. Use a wire frame if necessary.
3. Make a mask using gypsona.

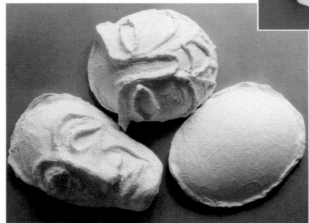

Faces and shapes made by students using plaster over balloons.

Moulds and castings

A **mould** is a shape into which a setting substance (in liquid form) is poured so that it takes on that shape when it is set.

A simple way of making a mould and casting
The mould
1. Make a clay tile in relief.
2. Place the tile on a non-porous surface.
3. Surround it with a collar of clay or cardboard. Seal it with clay or sticky tape.
4. Pour on the previously-mixed plaster and let it set.
5. When set, remove tile from the plaster mould.

collar of clay or cardboard

reverse mould when set

Casting
1. Coat the inside of the mould with **slip** (a watery clay mixture), shellac or washing-up liquid — any of these will act as **barriers**.
2. Pour previously-mixed plaster into the mould and let it set.
3. Sand or file down the back of the tile to form a smooth surface.
4. Remove the plaster tile from the mould.

Suggested Assignment

Design, make and cast a tile, or set of tiles.

Support Studies

Wax modelling

Wax is quite a specialised material which can be used for modelling. Melted in a double saucepan, the wax can be built upon itself. Candle wax is usually too brittle for modelling. Bees' wax is too soft. A mixture of the two can produce the kind of wax needed for modelling.

Two exhibits from the Dublin Wax Museum —Brendan Grace and U2.

Support Studies

Subtractive Work

Carving

Carving involves taking away material to reveal a shape or form.

Carving is regarded is as the most difficult of the three-dimensional Art, Craft, Design techniques because it does not allow for much error.

Planning is essential for all forms of sculpture. This is particularly true for any subtractive work. If a mistake is made, it is almost impossible to put it right.

Suitable materials for carving
- stone • wood
- soap   • plaster
- polystyrene

Before beginning to carve, think about the material and whether it is suitable for your planned piece of work. When starting to carve, remember to keep your design simple.

Stone carving

Stone carving can be traced back to prehistoric times. At Newgrange in Co. Meath, carvings were carried out with two stones. One stone was used to hit another stone which chiselled away the main stone. This was before the age of metals.

Signpost

See Line, page 73.

Until recently, all stone carvings were done by hand. Today, powerful disc saws with diamond tips are used for cutting stone in the quarry. **Wedges** (large chisels) are still put in by hand to break off large pieces of stone. Electric hand-held disc cutters and power tools are also in use now. These have taken alot of the drudgery out of stone carving. Power tools can be dangerous, of course. They are also noisy and cause vibration and dust. *Goggles, face masks and ear muffs should be worn at all times when cutting stone.*

Stone varies in hardness. Granite is one of the hardest stones. It is weather resistant and can take a very fine polish. Sandstone, on the other hand, is very soft, porous and easy to carve. Stone varies so much in its hardness or softness that special tools have to be used with different types of stones.

Carrera marble is one of the favourite stones for sculptors. It is quarried near Tuscany in Italy.

Carving stone is usually out of the question for beginners — unless you happen to be near a stone mason's yard. Even then, stone carving is very specialised and it may be difficult to get experience in this technique.

One of the world's most spectacular 3D (relief) works—Mount Rushmore, South Dakota, USA. The heads of four American presidents (George Washington, Thomas Jefferson, Theodore Roosevelt and Abraham Lincoln) were carved into solid rock. Each head is 18m (60ft) high. Dynamite was first used to blast away the surface prior to carving with traditional tools.

Working with Wood

Some of the richest examples of wood carving and sculpture came from tribal cultures. African masks and figures influenced many modern artists such as Pablo Picasso.

Wood is a very satisfying material to work with. Getting to know the different types of wood, their colours and their textures is interesting in itself.

When planning what to carve, you must think about the type of wood you are using — its hardness or softness, its grain, the tools you will use.

The design should suit the chosen piece of wood. Sometimes, the wood itself can dictate the form which is just waiting to 'break out' of the block. Many sculptors take hours to choose a piece of wood which is suitable for a certain design or plan. They believe that certain pieces of wood will contain the spirit of their work.

Wood Gatherer, Jackie McKenna. Beech wood. 1.75m x .75m (5'8" x 2'6"). Her first carving is now part of a sculpture trail in Hazelwood, Sligo.

273

When carving wood, it is important to hold the wood tightly and steadily — preferably in a vice.

A saw can save a lot of time in the beginning when roughing out the basic shape. Chisels and gouges are then used. Some sculptors often stop at this point and leave their work with a rough finish. Others go on to sand or file down the wood with small precision tools or with sandpaper. This gives the grain a chance to come through and become a feature of the piece itself.

If you do not have the facilities for carving wood in the traditional way, try carving with balsa wood. Architects usually use balsa wood for model making because it is very soft, light-weight and easy to cut or carve.

Safety first!

Always carve away from you to avoid accidents.

Care

Tools should be kept sharp and used only for carving wood. They should be kept clean and stored carefully.

Suggested Assignment

Collect small pieces of driftwood from the beach, or fallen wood from a woodland. Note the natural texture and shape. Try to identify the different types of wood.

Using sandpaper, sand down part or all of the wood piece until smooth. Observe the grain.

Observe and Discuss

. . . all the household items that are made of wood. Make a class display of as many types as you can. Collect pictures to add to your display.

Support Studies

Soap Carving

A block of ordinary household soap is easy to get. Make sure it is fresh and warm before working with it. Otherwise it will be too brittle for carving. All you will need is a knife and a good plan of what you want to carve. Cut carefully, or you could lose the entire piece. Do not bother with too much detail when you are just beginning. Keep your carving simple. When you are finished, wash the piece gently to get a smooth finish.

Students' soap carvings of lipsticks, clothes pegs and keys.

Suggested Assignment

Carve a small item from soap that has something to do with your chosen theme. Remember to make a plan first, and keep it simple.

Support Studies

Plaster carvings

Signpost

See Mixing plaster, page 270, before you begin.

Make a plaster block. Use any kind of cardboard box as a mould. It is probably best to start with something fairly small (5cm x 5cm x 10cm).

When planning your carving, first make a drawing. A detailed sketch with measurements is best.

Tools may be crude — an old knife and rough sandpaper to begin with, although you can purchase special tools for plaster carving. Hack-saw blades and old chisels and files also work well on plaster.

Suggested Assignment

Carve a block of plaster based on a given theme.

Polystyrene

The best way to deal with polystyrene is to use a hot wire to cut into it. Otherwise it might crumble and leave a jagged edge.

Polystyrene is not good for detailed work. It is usually used as a flat 2D type of medium. If it is layered, it can be built up and developed as a construction. Because of its lightness, it is the ideal material for a mobile.

Suggested Assignment

Safety first!

This exercise should only be carried out under adult supervision.

Heat a wire and cut into a piece of polystyrene. See what happens before starting on a particular project.

First, cut a curve and then a straight line. Then cut out a geometric shape. This will help you to become familiar with the material. Once you have mastered the technique, start on your own project or theme.

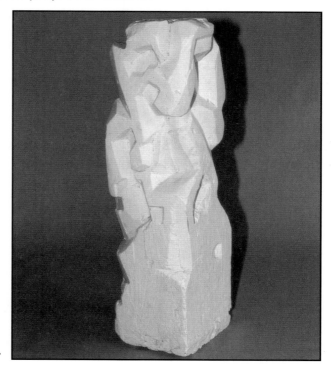

A plaster carving.

Support Studies

Construction/Assemblage/ Mixed Media

Just about anything can go into the art of construction. This is why it is sometimes called 'junk art'. It is very like a 3D collage and is often associated with 20th century modern movements.

Elephant, Bill Woodrow. An assemblage using car doors, maps and a machine gun. By combining these objects, Woodrow has tried to communicate his concern for the environment. Comment on what you think these objects mean.

The list of materials which are suitable for use in construction is endless. Here are some of the more obvious ones.

paper	buttons	lollipop sticks
cardboard	paper clips	plastic cups/straws
wire	clockpieces	chains
toilet rolls	wood	beads
match boxes	metal	plastic
bottle tops	stone	cans
beer mats	string/rope	egg cartons
coat hangers	cloth	pipe cleaners
feathers	corrugated card	sponges
wool		

. . . and the contents of waste paper baskets!

To put the construction together, use the following.

threads	tacks and nails	staples
glues	Blu-tack	pins
sellotape	double-sided tape	

Just a few of the things which can be used for assemblage work.

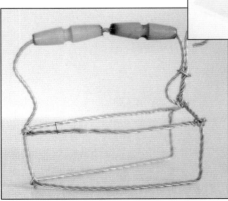

Students' constructions using wire.

Construction

Basic structures and joins

Take a flat piece of paper or card. Roll it up. Stick it together and you have a 3D construction in the form of a cylinder.

Making a 3D shape

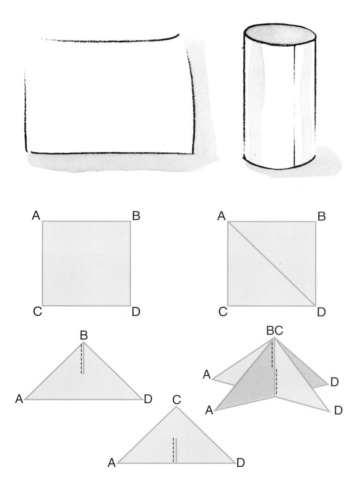

1. Take a flat, square piece of paper — a, b, c, d.
2. Make a diagonal from a to d — This will give two triangles.
3. Make a cut from b to the centre of the triangle abd.
4. Make a perpendicular cut midway along ad in the direction of c. Stop at the mid point of the triangle.
5. Slot the two pieces together to make a standing 3D form.

There are many variations to this approach. They can be used as constructions and mobiles. All you have to do is experiment. Make notes of your approaches and record what you have discovered.

Suggested Assignment

Construction exercises

1. Roll up some pieces of paper and make them into tubes/cylinders of different lengths and sizes. Stick or glue them together so they will hold their shape.

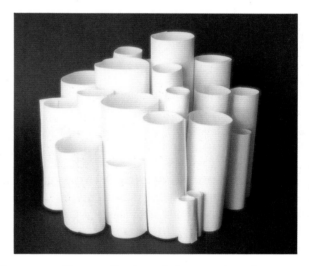

2. Arrange the cylinders into a pleasing composition. Try to balance them. There are many different ways of arranging the cylinders. Try it with the same lengths of cylinders but with different diameters.
3. Make a tonal drawing of your construction.

Signpost

See colour drawing, pages 27, 28.

4. Take another view of your construction. Use a lamp to create a direct light source. Make a tonal drawing of your construction and its shadow.

Equilibrium

When designing any 3D work, you must always consider its **equilibrium** or **balance**. Equilibrium is all about balance. Take a look at this desk lamp, for example.

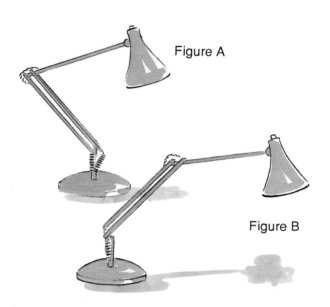

Figure A

Figure B

The only thing which is stopping figure b from falling over is the extra weight of the base. Even so, it still looks unstable — as if it should fall over. As long as the **centre of gravity** is compensated for, the equilibrium is maintained.

Most things that are top-heavy are in danger of falling over. Look at these examples.

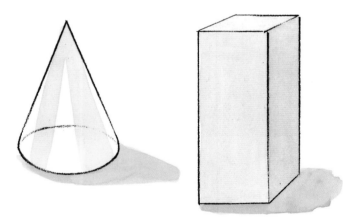

A cone is just about the most balanced shape you can get. If it is pushed, it will not fall over. A tall rectangle, if pushed, will fall over.

Observe and Discuss

1. Watch a child playing with building blocks. What happens to the equilibrium as the blocks are stacked higher and higher?
2. Look at the construction of a brick wall. Why are walls built like this?

Support Studies

- **When the material dictates**
  If you use one material only — such as match boxes or wood pieces — and arrange these in a regular way, this should be a quite successful construction. The shapes already relate, and the regular arrangement gives a sense of rhythm and pattern to the piece.

A matchbox construction.

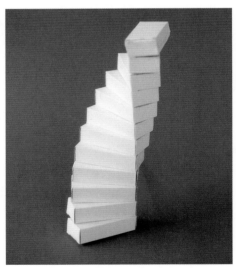

Signpost

See Pattern, page 43.

- **When the theme dictates**
  When a particular theme is given, it is always interesting to see how different people come up with different results.

Support Studies

Mobiles

Mobiles are sometimes called sculptures with movement. They are constructions which are usually suspended on wires or flexible rods.

As mobiles are constantly changing with the movement of air, or with the aid of a small motor, the viewer is able to enjoy a different aspect of the mobile every second.

Mobiles must be fairly light. Materials such as wire, sheet metal, polystyrene or plastic are often used. Card, paper, felt, florist's wire, cat gut (fishing line) or thread can also be used for less ambitious projects. These can then be hung from the ceiling using cat gut or thread attached to Blu-tack, a drawing pin, or a hook.

Mobiles are very popular in children's nurseries. Can you say why?

Suggested Assignments

1. Design and make a mobile for a young child's bedroom.
2. Make a mobile using 5 similar geometric shapes. Limit the colours you use.
3. Make a colourful mobile with about 5 – 7 letter shapes. You need not confine yourself to one letter — you may spell someone's name or the name of a theme.

Signposts

See Lettering, pages 192, 196, 210.
See Graphic Design, pages 188-241.

4. Invent 2 or 3 shapes based on a theme of your choice. Make a mobile with 7– 9 of these shapes.
5. Make a mobile which tells a story.
6. Make a mobile which illustrates your chosen theme.

Simply Red, Alexander Calder (1898–1976). Painted metal and wire mobile. Calder was interested in sculpture, engineering and movement. He is credited with inventing the mobile.

A student's butterfly mobile made with wire and dyed nylon.

Observe and Discuss

. . . the equilibrium of your mobile. Did you have to make any adjustments to the weight and balance?

Public sculpture

For the professional sculptor, the following must be taken into account when planning an outdoor or public piece of sculpture.

1. The reasons for the piece (commemorative, decorative, celebratory).
2. How much money is available?
3. What materials are to be used?
4. The location of the piece and the surrounding environment.
5. The size and scale of the piece.
6. The community — they are going to have to live with it!
7. Maintenance — if any. Who is responsible for this, and is the finance for it available?

All of the above will have to be considered when planning a piece of public sculpture. In the past, powerful rulers decided what a piece of sculpture was to be and where it would be placed. The people were never consulted. But we would like to feel that those days are over.

Today, cost dominates the whole procedure. tf often determines whether a work will go ahead or not. Costs will also have a bearing on what type of material is used — for example, the cost of bronze is greater than welding metal.

The scale and material of the piece, as well as the environment in which it is placed, may or may not complement the work. Costs will also determine the finish of the surrounding area.

Even when the sculptor is dead, the work may still remain in the community for many years to come. Vandalism must be considered. So must safety — are there hard edges? Will children climb on it? Is it dangerous?

Water in a city is always welcome. It seems to cool down the concrete and gets rid of the oppressiveness of the environment.

Observe and Discuss

. . . a piece of public sculpture, preferably in your own locality. Do you think it follows all the guidelines for public sculpture? What is the history of the piece? Who was the sculptor?

This 8.5m high (27.8ft) sculpture, *Circle of Time*, was commissioned by Hong Kong University of Science and Technology. It was designed by Australian sculptors Joan Walsh-Smith and Charles Smith.

Children obviously enjoyed this sculpture at the Glasgow Garden Festival.

Signpost

See Space, page 92.

Support Studies

Installation

A mixture of 2D and 3D

Drumbar, an installation by Patricia McKenna.

In this mixed media work, McKenna has created an environment which incorporates painting, photography, fabric and wood. The sheets dominate the work. They symbolise a bride, marriage, and death in the form of a shroud. All the other elements (such as the small framed pieces consisting of drawings, collages, paintings and photographs) give the viewer a further insight into the emotional aspects of the work.

3D Work by Students

A prize-winning construction in the 1992 European Schools' Day Competition. The theme was *European Union—No More Barriers.* Designed and made by 3 students at Ballyhale Vocational School, Co. Kilkenny.

A cat made with fabric shaped around an armature.

Cardboard clothes pegs.

Tree made with twigs, wood and wire.

Plasterwork cottages.

Sample packaging.

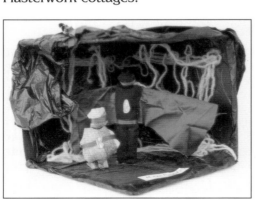

Assemblage of cottage interior.

A football stadium made from ice-pop sticks.

A boot made from wire and string.

Screen Printing

The Convent Window by Maureen Roche was created by using cut film stencils and opaque inks.

Support Studies

Screen printing is known as **serigraphy**. It is a relatively new printing process which began in the United States in the late 1930s, when it was given the name 'serigraph printing' ('seri' means silk). As far back as the 19th century, silk was used as the mesh to cover the wooden frame which formed the screen. It can be used to print on any surface — wood, metal, plastic, ceramic, paper, even glass.

Screen printing is a **stencil process.** The main advantage of using a stencil is that it can reproduce the same design many times. Stencils were used by ancient Egyptians, Romans, Chinese and Japanese. With them, they decorated floors, ceilings, walls, pottery and fabrics.

Signpost

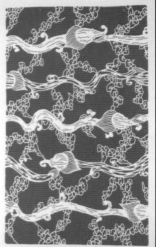

See Simple stencil prints, page 186.

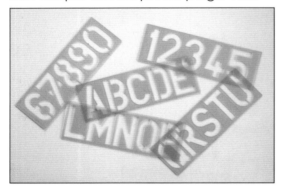

A plastic stencil like the one above was used to do the print for the packaging below.

Although these Japanese stencils date from the 19th century, they use traditional motifs which date back many years.

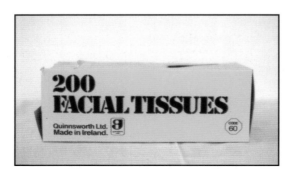

Suggested Assignments

1. Collect examples of various types of decorative prints from magazines.
2. Collect examples of stencil prints from boxes, packaging etc.

The main drawback of stencils has always been the problem of tying the floating areas of the stencil to the main image. We can see this in the following example.

The Japanese solved this problem by using human hair to join the floating pieces to the main stencil. Later, silk threads were used.

Stencils were first applied to silk mesh towards the middle of the 19th century. Silk screen printing was first patented in 1907. It used a stretched frame and squeegee. In the 1920s and 1930s, many new ranges of fabric design were printed by the textile industry using silkscreen printing. At this time, automatic screen printing machines came into operation. They could turn out thousands of pieces of printed paper at a time.

With the introduction of nylon and polyester meshes, a higher degree of accuracy was achieved. The name silk screen printing was dropped, and the process was referred to simply as screen printing.

Signpost

See Printing on fabric using a screen, page 296.

Support Studies

Raoul Dufy (1877–1953)

Raoul Dufy (Do-FAY) was a Parisian painter, drafts-person, stage designer, book illustrator, ceramicist and fabric designer. Although he was a friend of the Cubist painters, Picasso, Braque and Gris, his work shows more of the colour influence of Van Gogh and Matisse.

Dufy's fabric designs in silk, satin, cotton and brocade were produced between 1909 and 1933. His work is the basis for much of our modern fabric design today.

Dufy was also influenced by the arts and crafts movement of Japanese, Persian and tribal art which flooded Europe during the late nineteenth century.

Observe and Discuss

. . . the work of Van Gogh and Matisse and the way in which it influenced Dufy's work.

Fabric designs by Raoul Dufy.

The work of Raoul Dufy

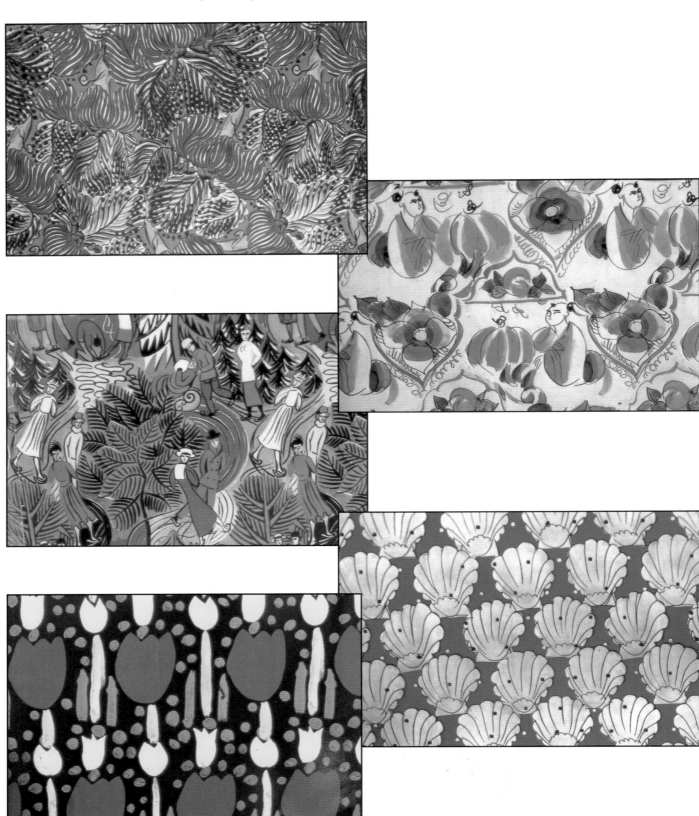

Support Studies

Screen Printing

Blaze, Bridget Riley (1931-   ). A one-colour screen print (black), 53cm x 54cm (20in. x 21in.). The Tate Gallery, London.

Compo Sta Ma Formosa, Venice, Bannister. Screen print. 20 colours. CCA Galleries, London.

Sweet Bowl (1936), a silk screen print by Patrick Caulfield.

Screen prints can vary greatly in style. This style is completely dependent on the type of stencil used and the **opacity** or **transparency** of the ink.

Opacity means that the colour is solid, and one cannot see through it. **Transparency** means that you can see through it. Glass is a material which is usually transparent.

In *Waves on Hook* and *The Old Oven*, liquid filler (a 'painted on' stencil) was used as a stencil medium. One screen and five colours were used in each case. The image was built up by overprinting one colour on top of the previous one. Some colours were transparent and others were opaque. *The Combine Harvester*, a screen print in five colours, was created using cut film stencils and opaque inks.

Waves on Hook, Maureen Roche.

The Old Oven, Maureen Roche.

The Combine Harvester, Maureen Roche.

Support Studies

Step-by-step procedure for making a screen print

Essential equipment used for screen printing.

1. Make a drawing of an interesting subject or theme of your choice.

Step 1.

2. Make a tracing of this drawing on art paper. One of the simplest ways of doing this is to place your work against a window. You could also use a light box. The light will make it easier to trace the image.

Step 2.

Step 4.

3. Paint the tracing in three or four flat colours, as the printing is executed in flat colours. These colours may relate to the original colours in the chosen image. The selection could be based on either harmonious or contrasting colours.
4. Trace out the stencil on newsprint. Make a separate stencil for each colour you wish to print.
5. Cut out each stencil with a cutting knife. Use an old, flat surface for this. Beware of damaging good table tops.
6. Attach the first stencil to the screen using masking tape.
7. Set up the printing bed using old, flat sheets of newsprint.
8. Register the paper underneath the screen by checking it through the stencil. Mark around the outside of the screen with a pen. Then lift the screen and mark the outline of the paper on the newspaper.

Step 8.

289

Step 10.

Steps 14 and 15.

9. Take a squeegee which is larger than the stencil to be printed. Tape the area where the rubber reaches the handle on both sides with masking tape. This prevents the ink from lodging in the groove.

10. Mix the ink according to the manufacturer's instructions. Water-based fabric printing inks are most suitable for the school situation. They can be used on either paper or fabric.

15. Catch the squeegee with both hands. Draw it across the screen at about a 45° angle. (Always remember to print in one direction only.)

16. Use the squeegee to return the surplus ink to the top of the screen.

17. Stand the squeegee to rest at this end also.

18. Lift the screen. Take out the print and hang it up to dry.

19. Take the next sheet of paper or print and register as before.

20. Continue in this manner until the required number of prints has been completed.

Steps 11 and 12.

11. Pour the ink onto one end of the screen.

12. Wet the squeegee blade in the ink.

13. Check that the printing sheet is in place.

14. If the screen is not hinged to a baseboard, get the help of another student to hold the screen for you.

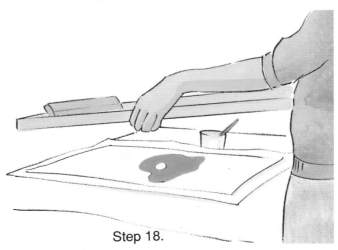

Step 18.

Cleaning the screen

1. Remove the excess ink and return it to a jar or can.
2. Strip off stencil from screen and place in the bin.
3. Wash screen and squeegee according to ink manufacturer's instructions. (In the case of water-based ink, some water and detergent are all that is required.)
4. Dry off screen and squeegee. Store flat to prevent warping. Never stand a squeegee on its blade as it will buckle.

The development of a skull print by a first-year student

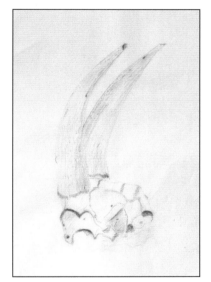
The initial drawing.

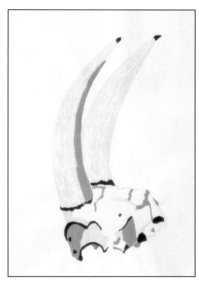
A 4-colour painting.

The first colour print.

The second colour print.

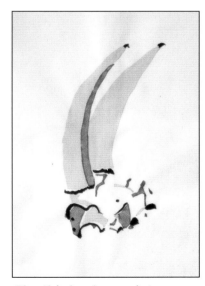
The third colour print.

The fourth and final print.

First-year screen prints

Pastel drawing.

Painting in 4 colours.

The finished print.

Pastel drawing.

Painting in 4 colours.

The finished print.

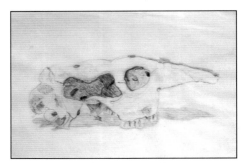

Pencil drawing.

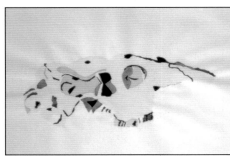

Painting in 4 colours.

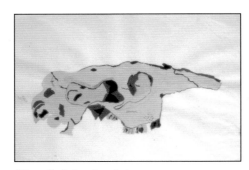

The finished print.

Second-year screen prints

Watercolour drawing.

Pastel drawing.

The finished print.

Pencil drawing.

Colour painting.

The finished print.

Pastel drawing.

Colour painting.

The finished print.

Junior Certificate level screen prints

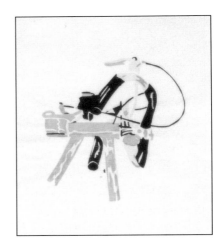

Suggested Assignments

1. Make a screen print based on your theme, using one colour.
2. Make a design to include an overprint. This will give you an extra colour.

Fabric Printing

Colourful fabric designed and printed by students.

Support Studies

Students will need these items for printing on fabric.

Dove, screen-printed cotton furnishing calico. Printed in England in 1935. Victoria and Albert Museum, London.

Printing on fabric using a screen

As in screen printing, paper stencils are only suitable for short runs of prints — fewer than twenty prints — or small amounts of fabric — approximately one metre. With long-term use, the paper stencil will absorb too much moisture from the ink and will start to disintegrate. For larger-scale work, use film stencils, wax stencils or photographic stencils.

The most suitable fabrics for printing are cotton, polyester cotton and calico. These fabrics absorb the printing ink well. Pre-prepared printing fabric may also be purchased. Ordinary fabric may need washing first to remove manufacturers' dressings.

On this page there are two examples of screen-printed furnishing fabrics. Birds portrayed in a semi-realistic manner have always been popular themes for fabric prints. In 1937, a leading manufacturer of dress fabrics in Britain needed as many as 800 designs per year to satisfy the eager customers.

Penguin, screen-printed furnishing linen. Printed in Northern Ireland in 1936. Victoria and Albert Museum, London.

The simplest patterns for fabric printing are either regular repeat patterns or half-drop repeat patterns.

Signpost

See Patterns and Grids, pages 53, 55, 56.

The size of your printing unit and the printing surface of your screen will be the limiting factors when deciding the number of units to be printed at one go. In a regular repeat, this can be one large unit, two adjacent units, or four units that form a square or a rectangle.

In a half-drop repeat pattern, either single units or two adjacent units are more workable. If space on the screen permits, four units could be used. While this will take more time in stencil cutting, it will make the job of printing much faster.

Water-based fabric-printing inks are the most suitable for your work. These inks are mixed with a binder. The lighter tints are very transparent, but as the colours strengthen, they will become less transparent. If an opaque colour is required, then opaque white must be added to the ink and binder.

With transparent colours, an overprint of two colours will produce a third colour. This results in greater versatility to the printed design. Of course, the colours achieved in the overprint will depend on the order in which they are printed. Yellow over red will give orange, but red over the yellow will only alter the red slightly. The same is true for blue. To get a good, strong green, yellow should be overprinted on blue.

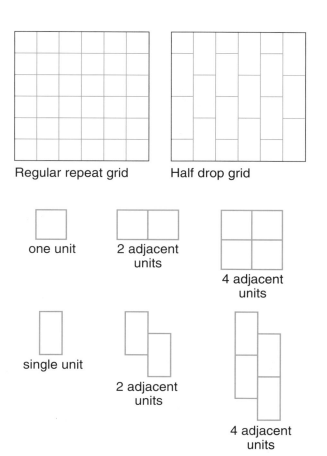

Regular repeat grid   Half drop grid

one unit   2 adjacent units   4 adjacent units

single unit   2 adjacent units   4 adjacent units

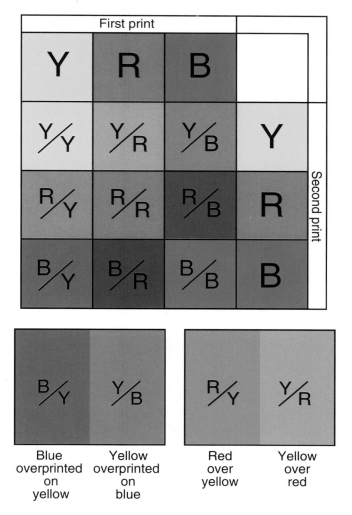

Blue overprinted on yellow   Yellow overprinted on blue   Red over yellow   Yellow over red

The fabric printing process

A fabric printing table is the most suitable surface for printing fabric. Very good results can also be achieved by using an old blanket on top of a flat table surface. Over this, lay some clean sheets of newsprint. The newsprint will absorb any traces of ink that penetrate through the fabric during printing.

Place your prewashed and ironed fabric over your printing table. Then measure up your grid. Always start at the selvedge edge of the fabric. The grid lines can be marked using either tailor's chalk or a needle and thread. Measure carefully. Make sure that the thread lines are taut and straight. Half-drop repeats will take more time, as all the horizontal lines will have to be measured accurately.

Registration

If you use newsprint stencils for fabric printing, the registration lines can be traced from the original design onto the newsprint. However, the newsprint stencil then needs to be placed against a window or on a light box to line the back of the stencil. These lines should correspond exactly to the lines already measured onto the fabric.

Print the darkest colour first, if possible. This will help in positioning the screen correctly for subsequent colours, as the dark colour can be seen through the screen. Always mark the stencil paper with the grid lines.

Prepare the ink by following the manufacturer's directions. Remember that materials will vary in the amount of ink they absorb. A very fine polyester cotton will usually need only one pull. A medium-weight cotton will need at least two pulls for a good, clear image on the fabric. Always mix enough ink to complete the pattern. It is very difficult to mix the same colour a second time. Some pre-mixed inks can be stored.

When printing, the ideal situation is to have someone else hold the screen in position while you print. This will stop it from slipping. (See the illustration on page 290.) Place pieces of clean newsprint over the printed area. This prevents ink from coming into contact with the back of the stencil. This paper will tend to absorb a small amount of ink and the image will therefore be slightly lighter than the printed colour.

Fabric printed by a student.

Registration showing how the repeat pattern lines on the stencil exactly match the lines on the fabric.

A student's fabric print.

. . . the T-shirts people are wearing today. Can you identify the different fabric printing processes used? See if you can spot a flat screen-printed T-shirt.

Individually designed T-shirts created for a Bruce Springsteen concert.

Printing T-shirts

When printing T-shirts, stretch the T-shirt on a stiff piece of card which has been cut a little wider than the shirt itself. This will give a good, smooth surface for printing. It will also prevent the ink from penetrating through the shirt to the other side.

The screen and squeegee must be washed as soon as the printing is completed. Otherwise the ink will dry on the screen and clog it up completely. Paper stencils can be removed quickly and placed in a bin. The screen is then immersed in cold water and washed thoroughly. In the final wash, add a small amount of washing-up liquid and lather the mesh well. Rinse thoroughly. Dry off surplus water with an old cloth. Store screens flat to prevent warping. Always store the squeegee with the blade uppermost.

The printed fabric is usually left to dry overnight. It is cured the next day. **Curing** is the process that fixes the ink permanently in the fabric. This usually means ironing the fabric on the reverse side for three to five minutes. Use a heat setting suitable for the fabric. As inks can vary enormously, the best recommendation is to follow the manufacturer's instructions.

Suggested Assignment

Make a design suitable for printing on a T-shirt based on your favourite pop group or a chosen theme.

Lino Printing

A lino print designed and made by a student.

Support Studies

A **lino print** is similar to a potato print. They are both forms of **relief printing** (the printing surface is raised).

Signpost

See Potato prints, page 179.

Items needed for lino printing.

Lino print Christmas cards. The card at top right was designed and made by GROW Kilkenny.

When making a design for a lino print, remember that very fine, delicate lines are difficult to reproduce. A simple design with good contrast of line and texture is more suitable for this medium. It gives a better-quality result.

Lino can be bought in a variety of sizes from most craft shops. If you choose to work with a very large piece of lino, it is best to mount the lino block onto a piece of wood. This makes the lino more rigid for cutting. The lino-cutting tools are small metal gouges which fit into a wooden handle like a pen-nib.

Lino blocks harden at low temperatures. This makes them brittle and more difficult to cut. The block can be placed on a radiator for a few minutes in cold weather before beginning work.

When cutting a lino block, always cut away from you. Keep your fingers well behind the gouge. The gouges are sharp and accidents can happen very easily.

A wooden support can be very helpful when cutting lino.

A wooden support can be used when cutting lino. It is a simple construction of three wooden pieces and is a great aid when cutting lino.

Practise cutting on a scrap piece of lino first. The grooves should not be cut too deeply. Ideally, they should be about half the thickness of the lino block.

When transferring the design to the lino block, use tracing paper. Remember to reverse the tracing paper so that the end result will read correctly.

Lino cuts can be printed using either water-based or oil-based block printing ink. Water-based ink is easier to clean up, but it can give a very flat, matt finish.

A boy's portrait: the lino print (left) with the lino block from which it was made (right).

A student's lino print of a tree.

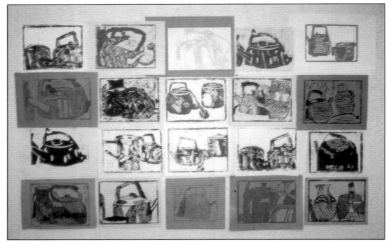

A selection of lino print kettles designed by students.

Making a print

1. Simply place some ink on a sheet of glass or perspex.
2. Using a lino roller, coat it in the ink and apply it evenly to the lino block.
3. Place a sheet of clean paper over the inked surface.
4. Apply even pressure on the back of the paper. A clean lino roller can be used for this.
5. Gently lift the print off by pulling it from one corner.

More than one colour

There are two methods to choose from when making a multi-coloured lino print.

1. A separate lino block for each colour.
2. A process of elimination, using the same block.

Note: Always start with the lightest colour (i.e. print from light to dark).

Batik

A detail from *Bestiary Beasts II,* a batik wall hanging
by Bernadette Madden.

Support Studies

Creating batiks

Batik is an ancient craft which dates back to the sixth century. It was first developed on Java, an island of Indonesia in southeast Asia.

The word 'batik' means 'writing in wax' in Javanese. In the art of batik, wax is applied to a fabric so that it resists the dye and thus creates a pattern. Batik was introduced to Europe by the Dutch.

In Indonesia, most batik designs have special meanings. The patterns are either random or regular repeat, with all geometric patterns being native to Indonesia. Free or random patterns are based on either Hindu or Chinese designs. Arabic and Indian decoration has also influenced their patterns.

When creating a batik, the hot wax is applied to the fabric using a brush and a **tjanting** ('janting'). The tjanting is a tool used for drawing in melted wax on fabric. It was invented in Java in the eighteenth century.

Daffodils, a batik by Bernadette Madden.

A batik warrior from Kenya.

The waxed areas of the fabric stay the same colour, as the dyes cannot penetrate the wax. Cold dyes must be used when doing batik. Otherwise the wax will melt. A wide variety of fabric dyes is on the market today. Just follow the manufacturer's instructions for mixing and use.

The fabric can be re-waxed and dyed many times. The end result will be harmonious, muted colours. The wax can then be removed either by boiling or ironing it out using newsprint.

The abstract batik piece on page 305 (bottom right) shows a piece of white fabric on which the batik technique has been used. The dyes were used in this order: first, aqua blue; second, jade green; and third, royal blue. The wax was then ironed out. This is just one traditional method.

Another traditional method for batik is to remove the wax after each dyeing and to rewax the different areas. This allows for much more variety of colours and overlays, but it is very time-consuming.

Modern fabric dyes, when mixed with fixer and dye thickener, allow the dyes to be brushed on. This means that a wide range of colours can be achieved.

Batiks designed by Junior Certificate students

Original colour drawing of a dolmen.

The finished batik.

The original drawing done with coloured pencils.

The batik which was based on the drawing.

The illustrations below show students' completed batik work.

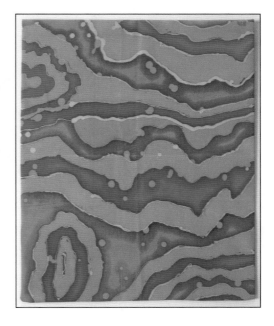

Materials needed for batik

1. Fine to medium-weight fabric with as high a natural fibre content as possible. Most dyes look best on natural fibres. Refer to manufacturer's instructions.
2. Batik wax is ready for use. Ordinary wax is brittle and will need some bees' wax added to it to make it more pliable.
3. Wax pot. *Safety note*: While wax can be melted in any container, it is well worth investing in a wax pot for safety. Batik wax pots are thermostatically controlled.
4. Tjantings or brushes
5. Suitable fabric dyes
6. Wooden frame and thumbtacks. It is better to stretch the fabric onto a simple frame, as shown. (An old picture frame would be suitable.) This makes it much easier to draw onto the fabric. It also allows the wax to penetrate the fabric better.
7. Old newspapers
8. For large-scale works, use buckets to mix the dye bath in.
9. An iron and clean newsprint

Never leave brushes or tjantings standing in hot wax!

Note: To achieve a 'crackled' effect in your batik work, simply scrunch the previously-waxed fabric before placing it in the dye bath.

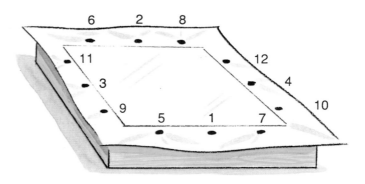

A wooden frame and thumbtacks (step 6).

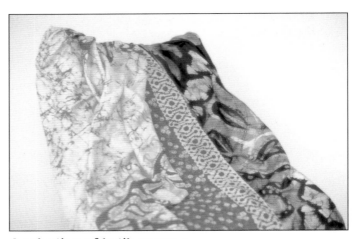

A selection of batik scarves.

Equipment needed for batik.

Wax mixtures

Special batik wax may be bought at craft shops. You can also make your own mixture of paraffin wax and bees' wax. If a larger proportion of bees' wax is added, the wax will be soft when used, so there won't be a very great crackling effect. If more paraffin wax is added, the wax will become harder and there will be more crackling. Some bees' wax is always necessary, as pure paraffin wax will crumble rather than crack. Add 5 tablespoons of bees' wax to 1 lb (450g) of paraffin wax. For more crackle, add only 2–3 tablespoons of bees' wax.

The Batik Work of Mary Lee Murphy

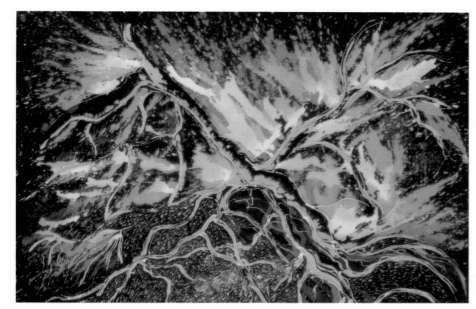

Fiery Trees, Mary Lee Murphy.

Slishwood II, Mary Lee Murphy.

Mary Lee Murphy was born in Waterford. Now based in Sligo, she works through the medium of batik. Her images are done on cotton, silk, linen and paper. She uses a direct dye application method, painting with dye and wax using brushes and tjanting.

The inspiration for her work comes from the landscapes of Connemara and County Sligo. Her work is energetic and colourful, as can be seen here in *Fiery Trees* and *Slishwood II,* both of which are executed on cotton.

Mary Lee Murphy has exhibited widely since 1985, both in Ireland and at Galerie Smend (a batik gallery) in Cologne in Germany. Her work is in many collections in Ireland, England, Germany, Mexico, Australia and New Zealand.

Creative Embroidery

Examples of students' embroidery work, based on the theme 'Cities and Countries'.

Support Studies

Embroidery is the production of ornamentation on fabric using a needle and thread to make stitches which result in patterns. The art of embroidery is a very old one. It goes back in time to when people used bone needles to sew animal skins together.

The embroidery which we know originated in the East. It was even mentioned in the Bible, in the Book of Exodus. Greek and Roman embroidery was derived from Asian art. The nomadic Arabs delighted in embroidering their clothing and even their tents. Rich and intricate embroideries were hung in the Kaaba in Mecca.

The early Christian Church used embroidery in pictorial form to teach the many people who could not read. It also enriched Church furniture and garments, which it does to this day.

Western embroidery was influenced by Byzantine embroiderers in the tenth century. Fine embroidery at the time was often reserved only for the Church and the nobility. Embroidered cloths were treasured by both the Christian and non-Christian world.

This delicately embroidered silk panel is from China's Tang Dynasty in the 9th century AD.

One of the most famous early examples of embroidery is the *Bayeux Tapestry*. It is 70 metres in length and about a half metre high. The stitches were made in coloured wool. The tapestry tells the story of the conquest of England by William the Conqueror, Duke of Normandy, in 1066. This section shows an encounter between Norman cavalry and Saxon foot soldiers.

The art of embroidery flourished during the Crusades of the twelfth century. It was used to depict scenes from heraldry, incorporating symbols of colour and design.

Many Crusaders returned home to Europe with fine examples of Eastern embroidery. Some of these cloths included precious stones as well as fine stitching. Banners and flags decorated with embroidery were used at tournaments around the same time.

From the thirteenth to the fifteenth centuries, embroidery guilds in England flourished. As embroidery developed in its range and techniques, it came to be used more widely on all sorts of clothing, purses, bags, buttons and gloves.

Some embroiderers of the seventeenth century copied the art of the sculptor. They often used relief in their work.

These three pieces of needlework show details of Church vestments. They date back to 14th century England, when embroidery guilds were at their peak.

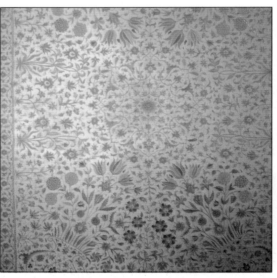

A sample of embroidery from Persia (Iran). It dates from the 16th century.

This delicate cotton floor spread was created in India in the 18th century.

Fifteenth century French tapestry, *The Lady and the Unicorn.*

In the Middle Ages, the inspiration for embroidered works was drawn from many sources. These sources were historical, exploratory, artistic and ecclesiastical.

Embroidery continued to develop through the centuries. But as mass production got underway, pre-designed transfers became more and more popular with the general public. Colour schemes were supplied with these ready-made transfers, so all the embroiderer had to do was the basic needlework.

Over the years, many fine examples of embroidery have been lost, either through overuse or lack of appreciation. However, some examples of fine embroidery from the past can still be seen in most national and local museums, in 'big houses', castles and cathedrals.

A hunting tapestry made in Belgium between 1425–1450.

A sixteenth century French tapestry.

Perhaps as a reaction to all this high technology, there has been a rebirth of interest in creative embroidery as a form of artistic expression. Once again, the artist or craftsperson is back in control of the designs, fabrics, threads and colours required for individual work of unique artistic merit.

Support Studies

Irish dancers are famous for their highly-embroidered costumes. Until quite recently, these were all hand-embroidered with traditional designs. Today, these costumes are machine embroidered, with different stitches available at the press of a button.

Ordination vestments embroidered by Maureen Roche.

Observe and Discuss

. . . the embroidered designs on these costumes and vestments.

. . . examples of embroidery in your area, especially older ones.

Church vestments may also be richly embroidered. Like the dancing costumes, the images may be symbolic, representing either Celtic or Biblical themes.

Support Studies

Tools of the Trade

Fabrics such as cotton (top left) and felt (top right) are suitable for use with traditional embroidery threads (centre).

Fabrics

Any fabric may be used for embroidery, provided the base fabric is strong enough to hold the whole piece together. Suitable fabrics include wool, velvet, linen, cotton, silk, satin, tweed, nylon, felt, polyester. A combination of different materials within the one fabric group can also be used — for example, light and heavy cotton. Of course, one must keep in mind that some fabrics are easier to manage than others. You will discover this after experimenting yourself and will soon come up with your favourite embroidery fabrics.

Felt is ideal for creative embroidery, even though it is a bit expensive, because it does not fray at the edges. However, it may also look flat and without texture, which may or may not be the effect that you desire.

Accessories for embroidery

buttons	zips	fringes
tassels	sequins	beads
fasteners	buckles	elastic
wood	plastic tubes	pipe cleaners
netting wire	metal	

Threads

Although there is a wide range of embroidery threads, you do not have to stick with the traditional ones. Before you get too adventurous too soon, however, it is a good idea to experiment with the more traditional threads when doing the basic stitches.

What is creative embroidery?

When embroidery is mentioned today, it usually gives us the idea of a pretty floral design executed from a transfer. But with the word 'creative', embroidery can take on a whole new meaning.

Creative embroidery is an art form which uses many different materials on a fabric background. It creates visual and tactile compositions involving a variety of stitches.

Creative embroidery covers a whole range of techniques associated with fabrics, thread and other materials.

A very personal and creative approach to embroidery can be developed if we take a theme and explore every possible aspect of it in terms of design and materials.

A clever use of accessories can lead to more creative work on any piece of embroidery.

Three different students created three completely different embroidered bikes.

Sources of inspiration

Drawings and plans may be obtained from both natural and manmade objects, photographs, newspapers, magazines, anything associated with your chosen theme.

One idea will always lead to another. Sometimes, the result will bear little resemblance to the starting point or theme.

314

Students' work on themes

Some sources of inspiration on which students could base their work.

Students' embroidery pieces

Observe and Discuss

. . . any hand-made embroidery work you have in your home. Find out who made it, why it was made and what it was used for.

Basic embroidery stitches

Outline stitches

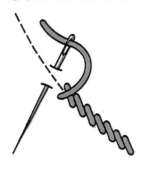

stem stitch

back stitch

split stitch

Flat stitches

straight stitch

satin stitch

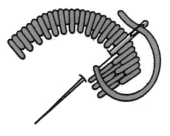

long and short stitch

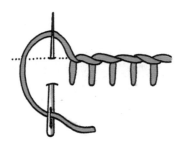

blanket stitch

feather stitch

Knotted stitch

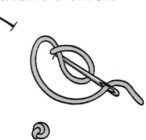

Chinese knots

Looped stitches

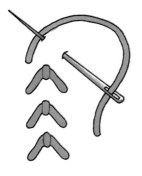

fly stitch

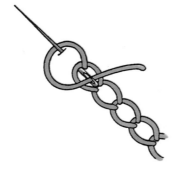

chain stitch

daisy stitch

Couching and filling stitches

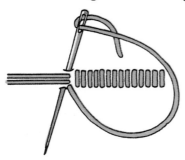

couching

sheaf stitch

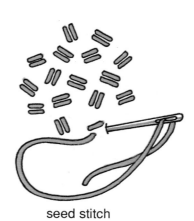

seed stitch

Canvas stitches

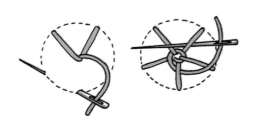

spider's web

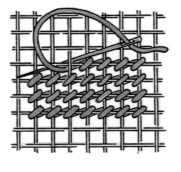

tent or petit point

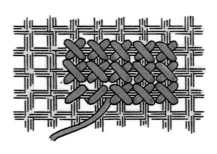

cross stitch

Making a sampler

Making a sampler is a worthwhile exercise when beginning to do embroidery stitches. It can then be kept and used for reference as you proceed. All stitches can be adapted and new ones learned as one gains experience. Using the same stitch with different threads or materials can also give a totally different effect.

Textures in fabric

Different textures can be achieved by using different fabrics. Some are rough, others are prickly or soft, hairy, scaly, cold or smooth. The suitability of the fabric will depend on the theme you choose and the effect you wish to achieve.

The use of different textures adds life to this student's church.

Different techniques

The way in which you use a fabric can change the whole appearance of the finished product. You can use drawn threads, appliqué, patchwork quilting (including padding), folding, cutting and smocking.

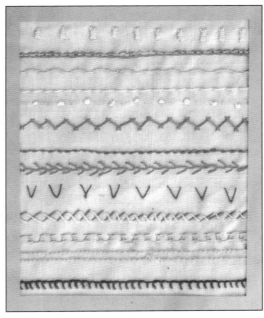

An average sampler by a first-year student.

Suggested Assignment

Make a sampler — it could be based on your chosen theme — using at least 8 different stitches.

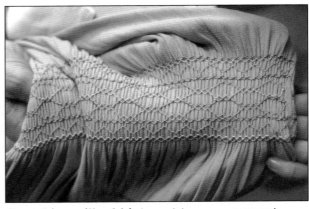

Smocking will add interest to any garment.

Students have given a 3D effect to these pieces of embroidery.

Students' work (above and below): simple weaving could be incorporated into creative embroidery.

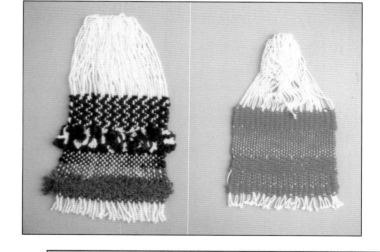

Three-dimensional effect

By adding bits of fabric and building up layers on other fabrics, you can create an embroidery piece which resembles a sculpture.

Other 'threads'

Wool, string, cord, braids, leather, even metal, may all be used. Don't forget that each of these 'threads' will need a different type of needle.

Suggested Assignment

Using at least 6 different stitches and at least 2–3 different fabrics (and anything else you wish to include like buttons, string, wire etc.), make a creative piece of embroidery based on a chosen theme.

Pottery

A selection of handmade pottery designed and made by Paul and Sue Taylor of Westport Pottery, Co. Mayo. Their beautiful stoneware is fired at 1260°C. Since all pieces are ovenproof, they are perfect for daily use as well as for decoration.

Support Studies

Pottery is one of the world's oldest art forms. Prehistoric humans made pottery. They used common clay to make various vessels and pots. The very earliest pottery was hand built. A simple mould was often used and the pot was dried in the sun.

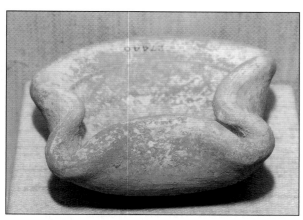

A simple pottery oil lamp from Egypt, made in the 6th century BC.

A fish plate made around 350 BC in Italy.

This Chinese terracotta army was made around 200 BC. It is so life-like that each warrior has its own unique face.

This terracotta creature was made in Mexico between 200 BC–AD 200. It was used to hold liquids.

Such pottery pots were often very porous — they absorbed liquid and sometimes leaked. This problem was solved by rubbing the inside of the pot with animal fat. Later, pottery makers 'fired' their pots by putting them in hot coals. This made the pottery less fragile and able to withstand heat.

Further developments came with the **pottery wheel**. With this, a potter had more control over his or her work. Things made using a potter's wheel are much more symmetrical and well-shaped than those built by hand.

Special ovens called **kilns** were then used for firing the pots. These kilns made it possible to maintain an even temperature. Then, coatings known as **glazes** were put on the finished pots. This made them very bright and much more decorative.

The ancient Greeks and Romans used pottery in their burial ceremonies. The Greeks recorded the major events in the life of the dead person — including the funeral itself — on their burial pottery. Pottery, not paintings, was used to record the Greek way of life and death.

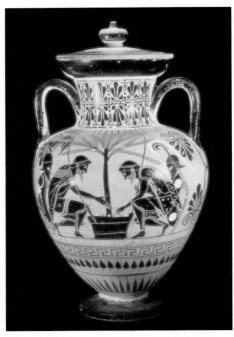

This Greek vase shows the heroes, Ajax and Achilles, playing dice.

A Ming vase with dragons.

A Ming jar with lotus flowers.

Many Greek pots contain scenes of battles and pictures of the many Greek gods and heroes. Their pots are often called vases. They were used to hold such things as wine and olive oil.

The Chinese have always had a great tradition of pottery. They are especially famous for a very fine kind of china called **porcelain**. Porcelain vases from the Ming dynasty (around 1360–1640) are particularly beautiful.

Chinese porcelain became so famous that the English started to imitate it. Today, our best cups, saucers and plates are often called 'china', or 'bone china'. Real bone china actually has finely-ground bone added to the clay. The result is a fine, hard, yet delicate and translucent pottery.

Observe and Discuss

. . . the Chinese terracotta warriors on page 321 and the Ming porcelain on this page.

During the Industrial Revolution, china was no longer made by hand, but mass produced. Colourful transfers and decorations were often used on mass-produced pottery.

A selection of Wedgwood pieces.

Often, no thought was given to whether this suited the shape and style of the vessel. The result was sometimes gaudy and lacking in taste. Factories often concentrated on technical perfection while neglecting design and decoration. As a reaction against this, the Arts and Crafts Societies were set up in England in 1880.

A few exceptional factories in Britain made mass-produced pottery. But they kept the old quality and were careful to create pleasing designs. Two such potteries were Wedgwood and Royal Worcester. These two potteries are good examples of the fact that, just because something is mass produced, it does not have to be badly designed.

The Dutch developed an earthenware clay which, when glazed in blue and white, looked like Chinese porcelain. However, it lacked the hardness and translucency associated with porcelain.

Most of the pottery we see today is made for home use. But this does not mean that its design and appearance should be ignored, simply because it is an everyday item.

Nicholas Mosse is a studio potter in Co. Kilkenny. He uses motifs which are drawn from traditional Irish images.

The Scandinavians were among the first Westerners to go back to pure form, creating a simple yet visually attractive type of pottery.

This unusual teapot was made in 1923 by Bauhaus designer Theodor Bolger (1897-1968).

The Bauhaus was a school of art and industrial design founded in Germany in 1919. Bauhaus members designed and made tasteful domestic ware for ordinary people. Their pottery was based on traditional lines. It gave a simplicity of form back to pottery. The Bauhaus was closed down in 1933 by the Nazis. But the tradition which it had established was carried on in many other countries.

Most pottery today is mass produced, not hand thrown. But many potteries now employ designers to ensure that the style of pottery made by a company is of a high artistic standard.

During the 1960s, many studio potteries sprang up throughout the Western world. This coincided with the desire to turn back to nature by becoming more self-sufficient. Because of its 'earthy' nature, hand-thrown pottery appealed to many people. Oven-to-table pottery became very popular. Casserole dishes, mugs and many other items were much sought after, especially when they were finished with natural glazes.

In 1965, the Irish government set up the Kilkenny Design Workshops to promote good design in Irish industry. As a result, many craftspeople, especially potters, set up their own studios around Kilkenny.

Suggested Assignments

1. Collect photographs of pottery from newspapers, magazines etc.
2. Try to visit a pottery if there is one in your area. Go prepared with questions which you would like to ask. Write about your visit on your return. Try to include photos or drawings in your report.
3. Find a craft or pottery shop near you. Spend some time looking at the pottery. Find out about the method, style and technique the potter may have used.

Pottery designed by Stoneware Jackson in Co. Kilkenny is made and decorated by hand. Clays and glazes are mixed to the potter's own recipes. All pieces are hardy enough for everyday use.

Materials used in pottery

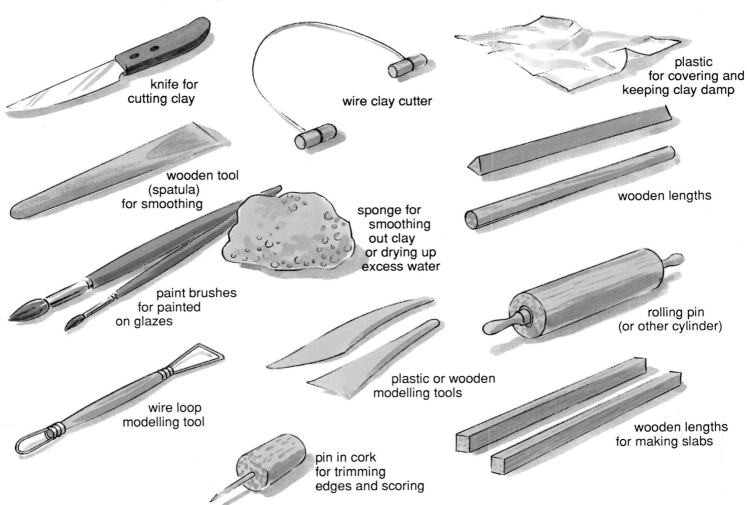

knife for cutting clay

wire clay cutter

plastic for covering and keeping clay damp

wooden tool (spatula) for smoothing

sponge for smoothing out clay or drying up excess water

wooden lengths

paint brushes for painted on glazes

plastic or wooden modelling tools

rolling pin (or other cylinder)

wire loop modelling tool

wooden lengths for making slabs

pin in cork for trimming edges and scoring

Schools which intend to teach pottery should provide the following equipment.

solid benches
kiln furniture
  (shelves, shelf props)
clay stores (bins with lids)
a kiln (with thermostat)
drying-out shelves
shelves or storage space for
  biscuit pottery
  awaiting gloss/glaze
  firing

Useful but not essential

containers for slips,   pug mill
and glazes, clays   potter's wheel

Each student should have access to the following tools.

- special pottery or modelling wooden tools (also in plastic) in all shapes may be bought or made.
- a wire loop tool
- cutting wire (twisted and attached to small wooden sticks)
- a knife (with a point)
- a corked needle (for trimming)
- a rolling pin or round piece of wood

Informal tools may be picked up or made from wood, discarded pieces of plastic, old pens etc.

Support Studies

A simple clay pot, with patterns made by a pointed wooden stick.

Practical pottery

Pottery making is one of the most satisfying of all crafts. In its soft, plastic state, clay is pleasing to touch and can be made into many different shapes.

Clay that is suitable for pottery occurs in many different parts of the world. However, the majority of potters buy their clay ready for use, in its plastic state. This 'clay' usually consists of a number of different clays blended together. Sand, grog or feldspar are added to provide strength.

Before starting a pottery project, you must become familiar with your material. The best way to do this is to get some clay, feel it, roll it out, make marks on it. Start with your fingers and then use some tools — or anything that will make a mark — a pencil tip, even a match.

The same pot in use as a plant holder.

Students can become familiar with clay by making patterns in small chunks or rolled-out pieces.

Clay varies greatly in its texture and the purpose for which it is suitable. Different clays are used for different types of pottery. The choice of clay depends on what you want to do with it and what effect or end product is desired.

Suggested Assignment

Try out different decorations and textures on a piece of clay.

Making a pot

Pottery may be divided into three sections.
- hand-built pottery
- thrown or wheel pottery
- moulded pottery

Hand-built pottery

There are many different techniques involved in hand-built pottery. The most common techniques are:
- the pinch and thumb pot
- the coil pot
- the slab pot

The pinch pot or thumb pot

This is a very simple technique. Simply roll a piece of clay into a ball. Then push your thumb into the middle of the ball of clay. Gradually work your way around it. Bring up the sides until the pot is formed. You may want to leave your thumb pot plain. You may also choose to decorate it with some indented patterns on the side or edge.

Making a thumb pot

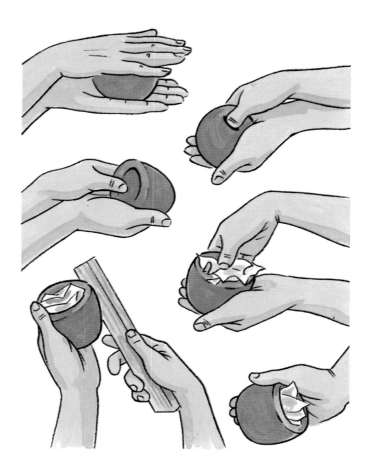

Thumb pots after biscuit firing.

A thumb pot after glaze firing.

The coil pot

This is a much more versatile technique than the thumb pot. It is built up with long coils of clay, one on top of another, then pressed together. Coil pots can vary greatly in size. The coils can be continually added to, depending on the base of the pot and the thickness of the coils.

The coils on a coil pot are usually smoothed over when the pot has reached the desired size. Sometimes, however, the coils are left visible on the outside for decoration. But this is not recommended unless the coils are sealed firmly on the inside. Otherwise the clay may split and possibly break at these points. Decoration may be applied on the smoothed area of the coil pot.

Making a coil pot

The slab pot

Making a slab pot is slow to start with, as you must first make the slabs. There are two ways of doing this.

1. Wedge the clay together in a block shape. Cut through the clay with a special clay cutter made from wire (like a cheese cutter).
2. Roll out the clay on hessian in between two lengths of wood. Keep the clay at the same height as the wooden edges.

Once the clay is in slabs, these are left to dry slowly until they are 'leather-hard'. This usually takes a day or two, depending on the weather.

When making a pot, work from a plan. This is especially true when making a slab pot, as the leather-hard slabs must be cut with precision.

Joining slabs must be done carefully or, like the coil pot, the slab pot may split at the seams. The edges to be joined must first be scored — usually with a fork-like tool to rough up the edges. Then, before assembling the slabs, add soft clay or slip to the scored edges before joining them. Work in the edges and corners to give a smooth and secure finish. Decoration may then be added. Slab pots tend to be geometric in shape — e.g. rectangular or cylindrical.

Making a slab pot

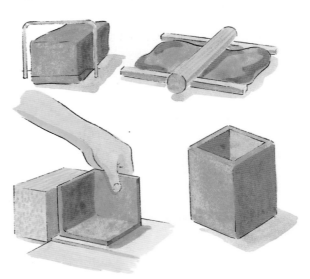

Thrown pottery (biscuit).

Students' coil pots.

Students' raised slab masks, biscuit fired and finished with shoe polish.

This slab structure was created from a cut-away cylinder. It was part of a student's chosen theme 'Wood'.

Thrown or wheel pottery

Thrown or wheel pottery needs a lot of practice before one becomes skilful at it. As its name implies, this type of pottery involves the use of a pottery wheel.

There are two types of pottery wheels: the kick wheel and the electric wheel. The kick wheel is more difficult to work with, but it is easier to gauge the changes in speed.

The clay used for the wheel is softer than the clay used for handbuilt pottery. Most potters add water to the clay when working on the wheel. However, continued flooding should be avoided. This weakens the structure of the clay and spoils the pot which is being made.

Wheel pottery involves 'throwing' and 'centring' a lump of clay. When you are putting the clay on the wheel, you actually have to throw the chunk of clay onto the middle of the wheel to make it stick. Otherwise it could slide off when you try to centre it later.

To centre the clay, you must work against the spinning motion of the wheel. This forces the clay into the centre and prevents the pot from becoming lopsided or uneven. The clay is then gradually pulled up to form a pot. Take care to keep an even thickness all around so the pot will dry out evenly and well balanced.

A potter's wheel with the 'thrown' lump of clay centred on top.

A pot being shaped by potter Brian Keogh.

Biscuit-fired pots being checked in a test kiln.

Firing pottery

Pottery is fired by being baked in a special oven called a **kiln.** Kilns can reach and maintain very high temperatures.

When the pot is completely dried out (this may take a week or more), it must undergo two firings. The first firing is called the **biscuit** (or **bisque**) firing. The pot is 'packed' into the kiln with other pieces. These pieces may touch each other. This allows many pots to be biscuit fired at the same time.

Biscuit firings (depending on the type of clay used) are normally brought up to 900°–1100°C. The whole process of reaching the required temperature and cooling down can take a day or two. The biscuit firing will make the pot strong, but it will still be porous. To waterproof the pot, it must be 'glazed' in a second firing.

Glaze is a special sort of glass powder. It is mixed with water to form a liquid suspension. The pot is lightly coated by dipping it into this liquid or by pouring it on. The pot is then put into the kiln for the second firing. This is called a **gloss (glaze) firing**. This time, the pots must not touch each other. So there may have to be two or more gloss firings for every one biscuit firing. The temperatures this time range from 1050°–1280°C, although this will depend on the kind of clay used.

Great care must be taken to ensure that the correct temperature is applied to any glazes which you use. The glaze must also be suitable for the type of clay being used. Otherwise bubbling or running may occur. Always let the kiln cool down completely. If not, crazing or tiny cracks could appear on the surface of your finished pot.

Moulded pottery

A simple pot can be made using any of the techniques you have already learned. A plaster mould of the pot can then be made.

Commercial potteries almost always work with moulds, although some of their work may be hand-finished.

At commercial potteries, a liquid clay is poured into pottery moulds. These are removed when the clay has dried. Technology is now so advanced that many of these pottery factories are fully automated.

Keogh's glazed pots with their painted bird motifs.

Press-in moulds

If you wish to make similar dish-like pots, you can used a technique called **press-in moulding**.

To fill the plaster mould, roll out the clay as you would for a slab pot. Then press it in gently into the mould with a damp sponge. Trim the edge to finish the pot.

For a textured finish, little ball-shaped pieces of clay could be put into the mould and pressed lightly together.

Moulded pottery is good for experimenting with different decorations and glazes. These pots are quick to make and are uniform in shape. This means that comparisons between glazes and decorations can be made easily.

Moulded pottery

This pottery owl was made from a mould designed by the artist Oisin Kelly.

In a book such as this, it is not possible to give detailed instructions for making pottery. We have only provided a brief introduction to the subject. But hopefully it will encourage you to work with this medium. Your pottery teacher will help you through all the practicalities. With practice, experience and time, you should be able to master the art of pottery.

Suggested Assignment

Possible Themes are given in parentheses.
1. Design and make a pot or container for holding sweets. (Food)
2. Design and make a candle holder. (Home)
3. Design and make a pot or vase suitable for holding long-stemmed flowers or foliage. (Home)
4. Design and make a cluster of pots or containers which could serve as a desk-tidy (for holding pencils, pens, erasers, drawing pins etc.). (My own place)
5. Design and make a cluster of pots or containers which could be used for holding jewellery or pottery tools. (Home/School)

Themes: A way of working

Themes are an excellent way of thinking and working. Once a theme is introduced, time is saved. Instead of trying to conjure up a separate subject matter every time a different area presents itself, a student will be able to draw upon previous investigations, flowing easily from one area or technique to another.

Approaching a Theme

Once a theme has been chosen, it should be narrowed down. Otherwise it may become diffused, losing continuity and unity. Here is an example.

Theme: Home

* **Brain storm possible starting points**—for example: house, garden, family, meals, food, rooms, housework, fireside, decorating, TV/radio/hi-fi, washing, clothes, relaxing, hobbies, celebrations, people, pets, visitors.

Starting Point: Kitchen

Areas of investigation (Preparatory Work)

* **Object Drawing — manmade and natural**

  table, chairs, sink, taps, cupboards, dresser, cooker, fridge, saucepans, cups and saucers, kettle, iron, food, fruit and vegetables, jars, plants.

* **Life Drawing**

  people eating, talking, cleaning, preparing food, cooking, arguing, laughing, reading (letters, bills, newspapers, books).

Support Studies

* Kitchen brochures, kitchen furniture old and modern, home magazines.
* Vermeer (Dutch interiors 17th century), van Gogh, Matisse, Cezanne, Picasso.

Approaching a Theme — Support Studies

Theme	Sources			
	Historical	**Natural**	**Manmade**	**Craft/other**
Environment narrowed down to **Flowers/Gardens**	Museums, galleries, art books, Vincent van Gogh, Georgia O'Keeffe, Still life paintings	Flowers, gardens, wildflowers, ponds, forests	Seed packets, garden centres, wallpaper, magazines, seed catalogues	Embroidery, flower pots, vases
Sea narrowed down to **Fish/Boats**	Archimboldo, Sean Keating, Paul Klee	Fish, aquaria, shells, seaweed, beaches	Fishing hooks and flies, nets, harbours, lobster pots, fish-plates	Cookery books, fish shops, fish as religious symbols
Buildings narrowed down to **Churches**	Churches, cathedrals, early Christian art, Dürer, Michelangelo	People at prayer, hands, funerals, weddings	Altars, chalices, candlesticks, benches, church furniture	Screen printing and embroidery (vestments), ceramics

Students' Presentations of Themes

Theme: Lips

Colour pencil study.

A pencil study.

Screen print.

Cut colour paper study.

Satin (embroidery) appliqué bag.

Theme: Fashion

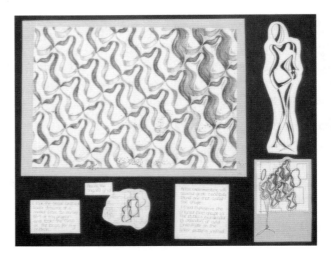

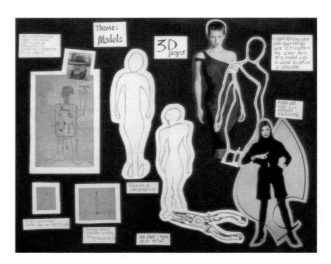

Theme: Cats (12–13 years)

Support Studies and Preparatory Work.

Investigatory sketches, Support Studies and 3D cat.

Support Studies, Sketches and 3D cat.

Theme: Wood

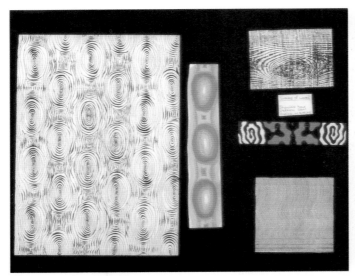

Pattern.

3D, Preparation and Investigation.

General research and Preparatory Work (12–13 years).

3D (15–16 years).

Theme: Cross (15–16 years)

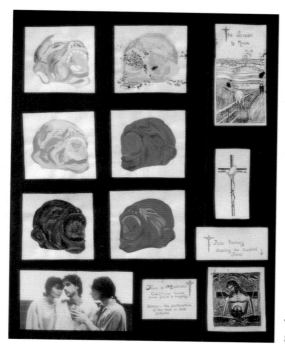

Tonal investigation of the screaming /crying head.

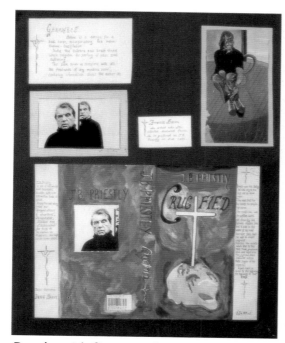

Dominant influence of Edvard Munch's linear woodcut *The Cry*.

Theme: War (15–16 years)

Modern warfare showing suffering and destruction.

Investigation of explosions.

Painting.

Record sleeve.

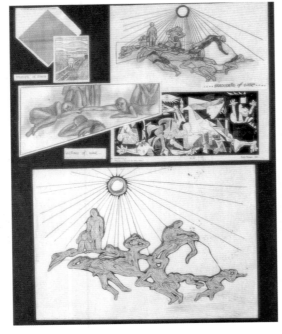

(Line) Painting.

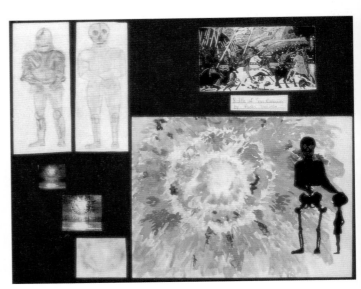

Explosion painting.

Different Themes—14–15 years

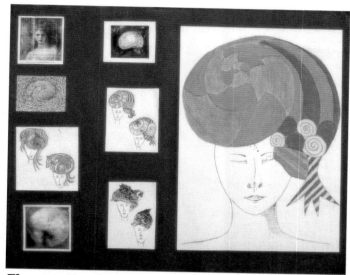

Theme: Headwear or Headgear. Support Studies and Preparatory Sketches.

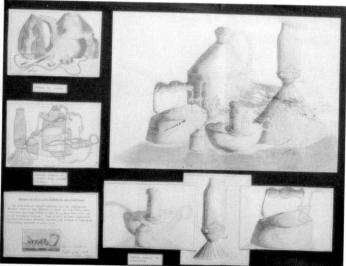

Theme: Kitchen. Preparatory work and in-depth studies—Drawing, Still Life.

Theme: Soccer. Support Studies and Preparatory (investigatory) drawings and paintings.

Index